STAND
daily

a daily dose of God's Word

Serve God
Love God
Observe God's Commands
Walk in all God's Ways

four 30-day, daily readings for
SLOW livin'

Ellen Harbin

Copyright © 2022 Ellen Harbin

All rights reserved. This book or any portion thereof may not be reproduced or used in any manner whatsoever without the express written permission of the publisher except for the use of brief quotations in a book review.

Scriptures marked NIV are taken from the NEW INTERNATIONAL VERSION (NIV): Scripture taken from THE HOLY BIBLE, NEW INTERNATIONAL VERSION ®. Copyright© 1973, 1978, 1984, 2011 by Biblica, Inc.™. Used by permission of Zondervan

Scriptures marked KJV are taken from the KING JAMES VERSION (KJV): KING JAMES VERSION, public domain.

ISBN: 979-8-9867314-0-7

SLOW Livin'
Houghton Lake, MI

ellenharbin.com

DEDICATION

STAND daily is dedicated to Beth Coppedge of Wilmore, Kentucky.

Dear Beth,

Your zest and zeal for
the Word of God deeply impacts my life.
Thank you for teaching God's Word with passion;
for applying God's Word with conviction;
for studying God's Word with intention;
for daily living God's Word with devotion.
To me, you are an original velvet hammer:
a beautiful balance of grace and truth.

Your life exemplifies how to daily stand firm in your faith and influences me to live as Jesus intends!

STAND daily / Ellen Harbin

CONTENTS

Acknowledgements / Introductions — vii

Book 1   STAND daily **S**erving God — 3

Book 2   STAND daily **L**oving God — 69

Book 3   STAND daily **O**bserving God's Commands — 137

Book 4   STAND daily **W**alking in all God's Ways — 203

STAND daily / Ellen Harbin

ACKNOWLEDGMENTS

I am forever grateful to those who shared their talent, expertise, and wisdom. Your involvement and support are appreciated.

Dianne Bogdan—editor
Brian Clark—author photo
    Captured Moments Photography, Houghton Lake, MI
Melena Cummings—Ministry Manager
Country Pines Printing—printing and production
Kevin Harbin—the one I choose to STAND beside daily

INTRODUCTION

The theme to this four-set daily reading was birthed years ago.

In 2009 I wrote and taught a Bible study about doing the right thing no matter what the situation may be. Throughout that ten-week course, the concept of *fearing God* kept coming up. Because I did not know how to describe it well, I went to God's Word for help. That is when He revealed something profound that still greatly impacts and influences me today!

Moses was leading the people of God through difficult and demanding days. Current culture is no different: Life is hard! We need God's way of living. Fearing the Lord is a part of His plan. So in Deuteronomy 10:12-13, Moses went to the people with a question, an answer, and an explanation.

Question: "What does the Lord require of you?"

Answer: "Fear the Lord your God."

Explanation: "Walk in all his ways, love Him, serve the Lord, and observe His commands."

The older I get the harder it is to memorize. I struggled to put this Scripture to memory, so an acronym was created: **SLOW**

In week nine of that ten-week study, I was diagnosed with a rare, aggressive, and high-risk type of uterine cancer. God asked, "Will you now live out what you have been teaching?"

Since then that simple reconfiguration of God's Word became my life's mantra, the name of my small business, and a mandate for me to live by.

Months after surgery, chemotherapy, and radiation, my husband and I took one of our sons and his friend for an afternoon of fun. Arcade, putt-putt, go-carts, and other activities were on the agenda. On the way there something inside me snapped. I went from being a sweet and fun wife, to being a snappy and nagging woman.

As soon as we parked the vehicle in the parking lot of that fun-land, the males escaped as quickly as possible which made me madder. I slammed the car door, turned to walk towards them, and I tripped. I looked down to see what caused my misstep. Painted in bold, yellow letters before me was SLOW. (The very picture is on the back cover!)

God spoke again, "Will you live out what you taught?"

To prove that God has a sense of humor, the fun-land was located three hours north of where we lived at that time. Last year my husband was assigned to pastor in a different community located in northern Michigan.

At the end of the street we now live on is the location where that very fun-land once existed. I now have a daily reminder to live as Jesus intends:

SLOW

STAND daily / Ellen Harbin

BOOK 1
STAND daily
Serving God

"And now, O Israel, what does the Lord require of you but to fear the Lord…to serve God…" Deuteronomy 10:12-13

Throughout the next thirty days each daily reading will focus on a Scripture with the word *serve* in it. Since there was more than one word used that means *serve*, if the word is from the Old Testament, it will be the same original word from the Hebrew language. Likewise, if it is from the New Testament, the same Greek word to mean *serve* is used.

Each day's reading is set up in the same manner:

- Title
- Key Verse
- Key Content
- Key Point

These daily readings are designed to encourage you to grow, challenge you to change, and influence you to live as Jesus intends:

SLOW

DAY 1

Fear Factor: Reverent or Scary?

KEY VERSE: *Fear the Lord your God, serve him only*...Deuteronomy 6:13

I recently heard a thirty-something-year-old woman say, "I used to avoid the Old Testament, but since reading it, I now see why you should fear the Lord. He can be scary!" Her prior perception of God skewed reality. Her avoidance created ignorance for her. Her newfound clarity needs explanation.

We cannot truly grasp what it means to serve God if we misunderstand or misinterpret what it means to fear God. Serving God requires we understand and accept Him as He is.

The character of God is not scary. But His corrective expectations for His children may be intimidating and daunting. And yet, fearing God is not about being afraid of God. To fear the Lord is to stand in awe of who He is—in wonder of His authority and ability, in adoration of His sovereignty and strength, in reverence toward His intensity and influence, and in worship of His great mercy, His amazing grace, His great faithfulness, and His constant providential care.

God is also relational and personal. He cares about you. He loves you. He is not unreachable or untouchable; distant or distracted; impatient or impetuous; reckless or rude. Rather, He is ready, near, kind, and gentle.

We cannot pick and choose which aspects of God's character will rule in our hearts. When we disconnect the relational side of God from the just side of God, we will struggle to serve Him.

Parenting can paint a picture of God's authority and model His strategies. When parents want their children to obey, it is common to tell children, "Because I said so." This is not always wise. Parents are not dictators; they are leaders. They are not authoritarians; they are examples. Christian parents should not be tyrants; they are tasked to teach and model how to fully trust God, follow His expectations, and obey His statutes.

Serving implies there is an authority to obey and rules to follow not because He is scary, but because God is relational and personal. We do not follow and obey God because we *have to*. Instead, we *get to* serve God because we love Him. We *get* to serve Him because He is trustworthy. We *get* to serve Him because we fear Him.

Serving God and fearing God go together. We serve Him because we fear Him. We fear Him; therefore, we serve Him.

Only.

It is in today's key verse and can seem insignificant, yet it adds a punch. "…serve [the Lord] only…" The directive *serve the Lord* is complete. However, adding *only* serves us well. A faithful God knows His children can be fickle. Instead of venerating we vacillate; we waver rather than worship.

To live as Jesus intends accepts Him as Savior, ensuring eternal life with Him. But Jesus says He did not come just to give us life (John 10:10). He also provides abundant life. And we do not have to wait until we are in heaven to experience and live life to the fullest!

To live as Jesus intends accepts Him as Lord, surrendering to His rule and reign over our life. If we desire to daily stand firm in our faith, we will submit to His authority. As we call Him Lord, we accept Him as our Master. When we yield to His lordship, we serve Him.

KEY QUESTION TO DAILY STAND: Today, will you serve your wants and wishes, or will you fear God and serve Him only?

Day 2

Is All a Tall Order?

KEY VERSE: *…but serve him with all your heart.* **1 Samuel 12:20**

The other day I went to the freezer to serve myself a mug of Rocky Road ice cream. When I noticed there was only enough to fill half the mug, I exclaimed, "Hey! Who ate all the ice cream?" Clearly, my snarky attitude had me exaggerating reality and misappropriating *all*.

All means whole. It is another small word that delivers a massive impact and requires our attention. In 1 Samuel 12, the prophet confronted the people of God, reminding them of His provision, protection, and plan. He told of how they forgot the Lord by recapping their sin against the Lord. Three times in the chapter Samuel commands the people to serve the Lord.

In his speech Samuel told the people how their ancestors forgot the Lord, ignoring His presence, promise, and plans and how they turned to false gods and sought a king when they had the Lord of the universe to lead and guide them. Many things attract our attention, and whatever has our attention has us.

Most Christians believe they are serving the Lord. They go to church and worship. They give their tithes and offerings. They pray. They attend small groups and participate in Bible study. They volunteer at their local church, in the community or on short-term mission trips. Each act serves the Lord. But serving the Lord is a matter of the heart before it is an action or deed.

Doing good things for God is not the same as wholeheartedly serving the Lord. For followers of Jesus matters of the heart, matter. In Ephesians 5:1, Paul commands, "Be imitators of God…" The word imitator means follower. God gave us something to follow: His Son, Jesus. Jesus gave His all; therefore, He is our example of how to give our all as we serve God.

On Good Friday, Jesus did not carry the cross halfway up the road to Mt. Calvary. He did not half-heartedly hang on the cross for almost all the sins of mankind. He did not forgive half the people who did not know what they were doing. He did not almost die; He wholly and completely gave up His spirit and died. Jesus was all in.

Halfhearted followers are not all in on their faith journey. When we refuse to forgive, remain bitter, or continue to participate in actions contrary to God's Word we are not all in. To serve God is good, but to serve Him with all our heart protects us from wandering off the straight path He has prepared for us.

KEY QUESTION TO DAILY STAND: How are you halfheartedly following God? What needs to change and what will you do about it?

Day 3

Gladness or Gloom

KEY VERSE: *...serve the Lord with gladness. Psalm 100:2*

Gloomy Christian. That should be an oxymoron. For followers of Jesus there is no room for gloom. A mindset shift may be necessary. Trouble will come our way, but it is not a reason to welcome gloom. Nowhere in the Bible are we promised easy living, though we are assured of suffering and hardship. And yet, that still is not an excuse to view the trying times as doom and gloom or expose others to a gloomy attitude.

To serve God well, we must trade gloom for gladness. There are many Christians with physical disabilities and difficult diagnoses: paralysis, blindness, limbless, cancer, heart trouble, and constant body pain. No matter the hindrance, gloom is nowhere in sight because they choose to serve the Lord in gladness.

In Psalm 100:2, the original word for gladness means joy, mirth, and pleasure. Anything we do in the name of our Lord requires it to be done with gladness. Psalm 100:2 continues, "…come before him with joyful songs." As we corporately gather on Sundays, our worship through singing, giving, listening, and volunteerism should be done with joy.

I also know followers of Jesus who wear gloom like it is a part of their daily ritual. Whether because of past pain, current reality, or worry about tomorrow, they make room for gloom. Have you ever walked into a church and been greeted by a grouch? There was a woman at one church I attended, who never smiled. She was in leadership, volunteering in many capacities. When I asked others about her glumness they would say, "Well, that's just the way she is."

Well, that is not right! Perhaps *she* attends your church or is in your friend group. Why does she get a pass to spread her gloom about the room? Why does everyone need to maneuver around the proverbial eggshells that she scatters about? The *"that's just the way she is"* is an excuse that is unacceptable in Christian circles, regardless of the church or ministry setting. Gently confronting a gloomy person loves them best and serves them well. A well-timed and creatively crafted question will get the encounter started.

Psalm 100:4 directs, "Enter his gates with thanksgiving and his courts with praise." Gloomy hearts are not thankful souls. Outwardly we can appear like we are glad, but if gloom is settled on our souls, then gladness is pushed aside.

People who know Jesus have every reason to be joyful and pleasant. Psalm 100 ends with motivation to serve the Lord with gladness. "For the Lord is good and his love endures forever; his faithfulness continues through all generations."

The goodness and faithfulness of God should inspire us to serve Him with gladness and influence us to daily live it out.

KEY THOUGHT TO DAILY STAND: Sullen and moody believers do not serve the Lord well.

Day 4

Serve Up a Helping of Humble Pie

KEY VERSE: *Serving the Lord with all humility of mind... Acts 20:19*

    I recently heard a sermon in which the pastor focused on himself a bit too much. He only used personal stories, examples, and applicational excerpts. He seemed to make more mistakes than usual by skipping past a presentation slide, forgetting a key point, and getting off his notes. I do not normally listen to this preacher, but this time even through his mishaps, though the sermon was Biblically sound, there was an air of pride in his delivery.

    Having a high opinion of oneself is prideful. The roots of pride burrow deep and negatively affect our walk with Jesus. We must all be careful to not feed or water the seeds of pride. We could all use a slice of humble pie.

    Whatever we do for the Lord, serving Him must be done with acceptable humility. Over the years too many ministry leaders made the news when they criminally, ethically, and morally fell. They forsook marriage vows, mistreated parishioners, and stole from their organizations. They stopped serving the Lord and began serving their wants and wishes.

    Talking about and paying attention to the pride in others is easy. But we must look in the mirror and see if we are hungering for and in need of a serving of humility.

    If we serve the Lord because it makes us feel good, look better, stand out, or elevates our reputation, we need a dose of the humility mentioned in Acts 20:19. Humility of mind has a lower opinion of self and completely depends on the Lord.

    When one of my sons was around eight years old, I overheard him broadcasting his basketball abilities to the boys gathered on our driveway. Before long the other boys left. My son came in the house as if nothing was amiss.

"Hey, son, why did the boys leave?" I asked.

"I don't know," he replied.

"Why don't you sit here and think about it a bit," I suggested.

Minutes passed and he responded, "I think they were just hungry, so they went home to get a snack."

"Son, they weren't hungry. They were tired of you talking about yourself and telling them how good you are at basketball. From now on, when you want to brag, you come to me. But before you boast, I get to tell you three things about you. And if one of my three things is what you were planning to say, then you lose your turn to talk." He took me up on that offer.

Prudence serves parents well. A serving of humble pie helped turn a prideful boy into a humble teen and a godly gentleman.

Pride begins as an inside job. Humility combats pride. Humbleness influences our service. To live as Jesus intends, we must serve the Lord as Paul modeled—with humility of mind.

KEY ACTION TO DAILY STAND: How can you humble yourself today and serve the Lord?

Day 5

Cleave

KEY VERSE: *Fear the Lord your God and serve him. Hold fast to him...Deuteronomy 10:20*

    From December 2016 to August 2018, we celebrated the marriages of our four older kids; three of the weddings were within nine months. The King James Version of Genesis 2:24 says, "…a man leaves his father and his mother, and shall cleave unto his wife…" I was profoundly impacted by the *leave and cleave* concept.

    The same word used for *cleave* in Genesis 2:24 is the same original word for *hold fast* in Deuteronomy 10:20. The Hebrew meaning is to cling, stay close, stick to, stick with, join to, overtake, catch, and follow closely.

    According to the Genesis account, to cleave a leave is required. Similarly, to hold fast to the Lord we must take leave of what has a hold on us. Deuteronomy 10:16 says, "Circumcise your hearts, therefore, and do not be stiff-necked any longer."

    First, we are challenged with a *do not*. Do not be stubborn. Be not obstinate or difficult. The Hebrew people had the same problem we have—stiff-neckedness. They were torn between their choices and God's commands. To serve God with our whole hearts, we must leave our way of living and wholly live as Jesus intends.

    Next, we are presented with a *how to*. Circumcision of the heart. Cut off, tear down, and destroy. We cannot wholly serve the Lord if obstinance, stubbornness, difficult attitudes, or actions occupy any soul space.

    Finally, the *how to* and the *do not* are followed up with *any longer*. It is like God is saying, "Once and for all." In other words this stiff-neckedness is not new. It is a continual cycle of rebellion, a persistent problem; therefore, do something about it.

Too many Christians are sick and tired of being weary, weak, and worn out! Well, maybe it is time for a circumcision of the soul and stop living stiff-necked. Perhaps they ought to do as Jesus said in John 5:14, "Stop sinning or something worse may happen to you." Or in John 8:11, "…leave your life of sin."

It is imperative to note we cannot cut anything out of our life by our own power. Serving the Lord well, requires we leave old mindsets, habits, attitudes, and actions to cleave to the Lord. Leave your old ways and cling to God. Cut off destructive habits and controlling mindsets and stick to the Lord. Destroy bitter, vengeful, hateful, and harmful attitudes and closely follow and stick to God's ways.

Whatever it is that keeps us from holding fast to the Lord must be surrendered to Jesus. Apart from Him we can do nothing; as we abide in Him, we leave our life of sin and cleave to our Savior and Lord.

KEY CHALLENGE TO DAILY STAND: What needs to be completely cut off from your heart to wholly serve God and live as Jesus intends?

Day 6

Revere or Veer

KEY VERSE: *It is the Lord your God you must follow, and him you must revere…serve him...Deuteronomy 13:4*

I live in a lakeside town with the curvy main road running alongside the largest inland lake in Michigan. Because the road is also a state highway, civil engineers designed a four-lane road with two lanes for each direction with no center lane. Today, as I was on my way to the grocery store, a car going the same direction veered into my lane. I slowed down to avoid the inevitable, while the other driver corrected his error.

The painted lines help us remain where we belong, but they are only guidelines; they cannot correct our mishaps. It is the driver's responsibility to respect and follow the laws of the road. Likewise, if we belong to the Lord, we must follow Him. And according to today's key verse, we must also revere Him.

We are back to the fear of the Lord: standing in awe of our Lord but also revering His judgment should we live contrary to His ways. Culturally, we want to highlight the love of God more than His characteristic of justice. When we separate certain traits of God from His character to align with our wants and wishes, we veer off His straight path. And when we veer, we cannot wholeheartedly revere.

Fear benefits us. Without it we are unable to properly assess and avoid danger. Fearing God is invaluable to His children. As the old hymn "Leaning on the Everlasting Arms" states, He keeps us safe and secure from all alarms. If we want safety and security that we can count on, we will fear God and follow Him.

A deep and abiding gratitude to the Lord ought to inspire us to serve Him well. If our motivation to serve God is to match and compete with His expressions of love toward us, we will spiritually veer. Love is the only motivator we need to serve the Lord. When we wholly love Jesus, we will reverently serve the Lord. Any other influence will have us veer rather than revere.

Swerving off His path veers our hearts in the wrong direction. Serving God requires proper reverence. God provides a straight path for those who wholeheartedly trust Him, who lean on His wisdom, and acknowledge Him in every way (Proverbs 3:5-6).

To revere God, we must follow Him. To faithfully follow Him, we must tuck in tight to Jesus. Serving God also reveres and fears Him. We do not serve Him because we are afraid of Him. We serve Him because we love Him.

Have you ever given a gift and received a thank-you gift in return? How do you respond to that—send a thank-you present for the thank-you gift? When does it end? A gift is given to communicate gratefulness or celebration. They are to be used, enjoyed, and benefit the recipient. As we participate in competitive gifting a precedent is set, and along the way, we veer from the original intent.

KEY POINT TO DAILY STAND: It is your choice: revere or veer; swerve or serve.

Day 7

J.O.Y.

KEY VERSE: *Serve wholeheartedly, as if you were serving the Lord, not men.* **Ephesians 6:7**

In today's Christian culture we are deceived to believe certain mantras. One resounding refrain broadcasts *you are enough.*
It is a lie.
This pervasive message has infiltrated the Body of Christ. Truth is, either you are enough or Jesus is enough. It cannot go both ways. The problem is the first word—you. The trifecta of me, myself, and I is a stumbling block to serving Jesus right and well.
Thinking we are enough has *eyes on self.* We cannot see, nor meet the needs of others with our eyes on ourselves.

J-O-Y, J-O-Y
That must surely be
Jesus first, **Y**ourself last, and **O**thers in between.

It is unclear who to credit for this little ditty I learned as a child. Regarding serving, it simply states our intended position. Theologically, it may need refining, but the point is communicated: Get our eyes off ourselves, look to Jesus, serve others, and know joy!
But the fact is there are difficult people in our lives— at our churches, in our communities, even in our families. But as Paul says in our theme verse, if we are serving with an all-in mindset and attitude when we serve people, we do it as if they were Jesus Himself.
Hebrews 12:2 asserts, "Let us fix our eyes on Jesus…" Though the cross is our symbol of salvation, we are incapable of being cross-eyed. The original meaning of the

word *fix* is a two-step process. First, we must look away from what has our attention, as if turning our back to it, and then intentionally look to Jesus.

I have seen a few people use *cross-eyed* before their signature on an email or letter. Keeping the cross of Jesus before us keeps our gaze in the right direction. It positively affects motivation, inspiration, and servitude.

Hebrews 12:2 goes on, "…who for the joy set before him endured the cross…" Jesus was all-in on His cross. Therefore, He is our example of how we live as Jesus intends: All in, *and* with joy!

This includes serving others. God will reveal the needs of others so we can serve them right and well. If we are *cross-eyed* and fixed on Jesus, then we will see *the others* we are to serve through His gaze and serve them wholeheartedly—with joy!

KEY CONSIDERATION TO DAILY STAND: How do you respond when God opens another's eyes to see and meet your needs?

Day 8

The Reign Determines the Rain

KEY VERSE: *…discern between the one who serves God and the one who does not. Malachi 3:18*

Corruption and chaos seem to reign around us. But in Isaiah 45:8, the prophet speaks for God, "…rain down righteousness…let righteousness grow…" Too many followers of Jesus focus on the reign of doom rather than God's rain of righteousness.

Disciples of Jesus are to please God, not align with culture. Many believers are confused as they trade God's statutes for cultural standards. A battle of the mind and a war of the soul wage a fight for a follower's allegiance.

Malachi was a prophet of God, sent to confront and correct God's people. They doubted God's covenant, distrusted His justice, dishonored their mandates for worship, lost hope, were unfaithful, and kept what belonged to God. They needed correction!

We all do.

Jesus said, "If you belonged to the world, it would love you as its own. As it is, you do not belong to the world, but I have chosen you out of the world…" (John 15:19). We are either in Christ or in the world. Our souls are not made to divide and dwell in both.

If your character, attitude, and lifestyle were placed in a line-up with non-Christians, could you be identified as righteous? What if your video streaming choices and reading material were in the same line-up?

Some think it is nobody's business how we conduct ourselves behind closed doors. But that is not true—how we live matters. One of the last things Jesus did after His resurrection and before His ascension was communicate the Great Commission for all His followers.

"Go and make disciples…" (Matthew 28:19). It means to help others to mature and grow as disciples of Jesus; develop a lifestyle as a disciple; to instruct and help them in belief and practice.

There is a distinction between the righteous and the unrighteous. And it should be noticed. God's Word is filled with statutes and decrees and commands on how to live. But when we blur the lines between what His Word says and what we want it to mean, it is difficult to discern righteousness from unrighteousness.

Discernment is not judgmental; rather, it is prudent to make the distinction so we can fully obey the Great Commission.

Volunteerism is one avenue to making disciples. It is vital that we understand that all volunteering opportunities are acts of service to the Lord. As we serve in positions, we help meet the needs of the church and the people, but ultimately, we serve God.

Because God sees our motives and intentions, we can be assured He is making the distinction between what acts of service are righteous and which ones are not. If you were willing to live in a glasshouse, how many disciples would get made from watching your everyday life?

KEY POINT TO DAILY STAND: If cultural standards reign, there will be no rain of righteousness.

Day 9

Bound to a Brick

KEY VERSE: *…by dying to what once bound us…we serve in the new way of the Spirit…Romans 7:6*

My son and his wife have two dogs, Rex and Fitz. When I pulled into their driveway the other day, Rex started toward me, but he could only advance so far. I got out of my car, walked to where he was waiting to greet me, stooped to pet him, and noticed his cable lead was attached to a small brick sitting on the lawn.

After a simple inquiry to my son, he informed me Rex thinks he is unable to move beyond the spot where the lead starts to tug on his collar. Based on his size and strength, Rex could easily drag the brick wherever he wanted with the lead still attached to his collar. But he remains bound to the brick.

Like Rex, there are things that hold us back from experiencing freedom and release. Freedom from past bonds and chains; release from old methods and patterns.

In July of 2018, Jesus called my sweet mom home to glory. In my living room is a framed photograph of her and her Pop with *Princess* bedazzled on the border. My grandpa was not her biological father, but he was the dad God provided.

When mom was a young girl, her birth father told her she would never amount to anything, and she would remain stupid for the rest of her life. She was bound to those devastating declarations.

Until Pop came along. Mom was fifteen when grandma introduced her to Robert.

Grandma said, "Robert, this is my daughter Linda."
Robert replied, "Well hello, Princess."
And he called her that for the next fifty-four years

until Jesus called him home.

Freedom and release. Freed from the bonds of brokenness began, the old cadence of unworthiness was interrupted, and a release of hope sprung to life in a fifteen-year-old girl.

A few years later mom gave her life to Jesus, married my dad, and raised three girls. I witnessed my mom serve the Lord in many capacities. One would never know she was once so broken and bound to such meanness.

Mom volunteered as a Sunday School teacher, a Vacation Bible School helper, a camp counselor, and an adult youth sponsor. She sang in the church choir, participated in the bell choir, and at times, played her coronet. She was active in women's ministry, made meals for those in need, sewed costumes for children's performances, and helped in the kitchen during events.

Every act of service to the Lord was not done through old means and mindsets; she served Jesus because the Spirit refreshed her soul when He entered her life.

One brick cannot build a wall. But many can make a fortress around a heart. Only Jesus can break down the bricks of shame, guilt, pride, unworthiness, hatred, unacceptance, and all that keeps us bound and held back from truly serving Him.

KEY CONSIDERATION TO DAILY STAND: What bricks stand in the way of you fully surrendering to Jesus and serving the Lord?

Day 10

Wander Well

KEY VERSE: *…let my people go, that they may serve me in the wilderness…Exodus 7:16*

The New International Version says, "…that they may worship me in the desert…" A wilderness or desert gets interpreted as a wasteland. But as it has been said, God does not waste a wasteland.

Followers of Jesus can be led into a wilderness by the Lord, or they can be misled by Satan. If God leads us in, there will be purpose and promise as He will not allow it to be a waste for our faith journey. But if Satan tempts us in and we follow His deception, we can be assured it will be a wasteland filled with heartache and hurt.

In the Exodus account, as God's mouthpiece, Moses is pleading with the Pharaoh to let His people go. God's people have been in captivity in Egypt long enough. It is time for them to go to the Promised Land. But in between bondage and promise is the wilderness.

Along our walk with Jesus, we will enter, dwell, and live through many wilderness experiences. According to our theme verse, God is demanding the release of His people from custody and confinement to be led to the wilderness, proving at times, he leads us to the space in between.

If we are praying for escape, we will miss God's intent. If we are avoiding the accompanying hardships, we cannot see His wonder-working power. If we lose faith in Him, it will weigh heavy on our hearts and minds. If we stop taking the Lord at His Word, we will waste the opportunity to grow deeper roots in Jesus. If we doubt His presence, we will experience His provision or witness His protection.

God calls us to the wilderness to serve Him. He leads us to the desert to worship Him. It is in the dried-up places and the uninhabited spaces of our soul that God desires to dwell and commune. But He will not storm those gates or rush in without invitation.

Though He promises to be with us in the wilderness, He will lead us in as we take hold of His hand. If we stubbornly stand on the threshold, though He beckons us in, He will not force our following.

And yet, life goes on. Hardship happens and crises come whether we are ready or not. We should be prepared for the wilderness before we are standing at the edge. We cannot wander well until we are tucked in tight to Jesus. And we cannot stand firm until we stand on the premises and promises of God's Word.

Standing on the edge of the wilderness is like the foolish man who built his house upon the sand (Luke 6:46-49). When the rains came and the floods rose, the house on the sand went splat! But when we trust God in the wilderness, crossing the threshold is like the wise man who built his house on the Solid Rock. Due to the sturdy foundation, nothing could take it down.

KEY QUESTION TO DAILY STAND: What needs to happen on your walk of faith to wander well in the wilderness?

Day 11

WWJD

KEY VERSE: *...It is the Lord Christ you are serving. Colossians 3:24*

Years ago, a popular acronym swept our nation. WWJD was created by a youth director in Holland, MI, but inspired by Charles Sheldon's book, *In His Steps*. The acronym was first displayed on bracelets to remind the teens of that youth group to consider *What Would Jesus Do?*

In preparation for today's writing, I went back and started reading the beginning of Colossians chapter three. I did not get far, as one verb in my New International Version Bible stood out. The same verb was used twice in the first two verses.

Paul writes, "...set your hearts on things above...Set your minds on things above..."

Action words grab my attention, especially those in God's Word. The English words used to translate the original language of the Old and New Testaments are sufficient, but at times, the Spirit of God reveals a deeper understanding.

Translators of my Bible chose the same English verb, but the original manuscript uses two different verbs. (And many English translations do as well.) In Colossians 3:1, the Greek word for set is zéteó. And in Colossians 3:2, it is phroneó.

Zéteó means to seek by inquiring, to investigate, and search. It is to get to the bottom of a matter. Like many foreign languages, the word phroneó is difficult to translate because the one word combines two differing aspects: knowing and instinct. It is opinion fleshed out in action.

Paul charges Christians to search out and seek, inquire and investigate, and to not give up until their hearts are set where they should be. But Paul knows our minds can carry us away. We are prone to wander when we trust our thinking and feeling over God's truth. We are led astray when we trust feeling over fact. We are not meant to be emotionally, mentally, or spiritually pulled in two directions, so Paul directs our minds away from earthly things. He instructs that we align our affections in one direction: heavenward.

Giving more attention and affection to the things of the world weakens our devotion, wearies our resolve, and leaves us worn out. How do we live in the world but think about things above when the world vies for our attention and coerces our affections?

Crossroads of temptation or trouble, the proverbial fork-in-the-road, the edge of a cliff, or hanging by a thread, are all brinks of spiritual decline or disaster. They have us focused on *What am I going to do? What is the way out? Why did this happen? How did I get here?*

WWJD. It may seem cliché or trite, but what would Jesus do? Because God's Word instructs it; instead of thinking about what you can do, set your mind and heart on what Jesus would do. Every time we get our focus back on Jesus, we serve Him. After all, *it is the Lord Christ you are serving.*

KEY ASSIGNMENT TO DAILY STAND: Today I will ponder WWJD as I set my heart and mind on things above.

Day 12

Hard Truth

KEY VERSE: *…only fear the Lord and serve him in truth… 1 Samuel 12:24*

We tend to avoid hard decisions and experiences because somehow, we have been deceived to believe that hard is bad. Someone once shared a painful experience with me. She ended, "Ellen, it's just hard!" I responded, "Hard isn't bad. It's just hard." The truth is, at times, we all need hard truth.

Samuel was a prophet. God appointed and ordained him to lead His people, the Israelites. There came a time when God had a message for Samuel to deliver. It was the truth and it was hard to hear, but it was necessary. The people had neglected and abandoned God. They needed His intervention and help to get them back on their spiritual journey—to walk by faith and not by sight.

In 1 Samuel chapter twelve, the prophet is giving his last speech. He backs the train up and reminds the people where they and their forefathers had spiritually derailed. Yes, our sin affects us, but those sins and the sins of our ancestors can and will affect future generations as well. We must stay on track; otherwise, we contribute to our lineage wreckage.

The people bypassed God as their Supreme Authority and demanded Samuel appoint a king to lead them *such as all the other nations have* (1 Samuel 8:5). This is one example from yesterday's reading on having our eyes on earthly things. Demanding our will be done will have us undone.

As a mouthpiece for God, Samuel spoke hard truth. "If you fear the Lord and serve and obey him and do not rebel against his commands, and if both you and the king who reigns over you follow the Lord your God—good! But if you do not obey the Lord, and if you rebel against his commands, his hand will be against you, as it was against your fathers" (1 Samuel 12:14-15).

Hard to hear; simple to understand. It requires intentionality to live out; yet it is easy to derail. Samuel followed the hard truth with, "Do not turn away after useless idols," and "I will teach you the way that is good and right" (1 Samuel 12:21 & 23).

- Be sure to fear the Lord.
- Serve Him in truth, or faithfully.
- Consider what great things He has done for you.

There it is! Three steps from 1 Samuel 12:24 for living good and right. We make following Jesus and living as he intends difficult. God already has the way paved; the path straight; the tracks sturdy and steadfast.

But Samuel did not leave God's people undone without more hard truth. It is our choice if we faithfully follow, but like Samuel told the people, know there are consequences for disconnecting from God's will, disobeying His ways, and derailing off the straight track He provides.

"Yet, if you persist in doing evil, both you and your king will be swept away" (1 Samuel 12:25). We can be carried away and consumed by sin—when we persist in it. Being captured and snatched by evil has grave consequences—for you and your descendants. Therefore, listen to and receive the hard truth. It will serve you well so you can serve the Lord in truth.

KEY QUESTION TO DAILY STAND: Do you bristle at or bear the hard truth?

Day 13

Devotion

KEY VERSE: *No one can serve two masters...Matthew 6:24*

Money is *not* the root of all evil.
It has been taught, but until it is caught, it must be retaught. Money itself is not evil, the *love* of it is. If we belong to Jesus, He is our Master. If money masters us, we are devoted to it. Plain and simple.

Jesus says, "No one can serve two masters…he will be devoted to the one and despise the other. You cannot serve both God and money" (Matthew 6:24). Other versions use mammon, wealth, gold, or worldly riches. The original word means *the treasure a person trusts in*.

The financial climate today is fickle and capricious. Perusing the terms of retirement portfolios is perplexing and unsettling. The housing market is ever-changing. Over the past few months, grocery bills have nearly doubled.

Yes, our cash is deposited and held in banks, our investments are in mutual funds and the market, our pensions and social security benefits have government or corporate oversight.

If that last paragraph brought heartburn or heartache, a service check is in order. It is prudent to know the performance of your financial state, but if it leaves us mentally reeling and emotionally unsteady, it will have us spiritually shaken, our devotion in question.

There is good news for followers of Jesus. When we fear the Lord and completely serve Him, we give Him permission to operate and manage what He already owns.

Psalm 50:10 says, "…for every animal of the forest is mine, and the cattle on a thousand hills." God owns it all, but he shares it with humanity. For Christians, His children, it is up to us if we will allow Him to rule and reign over all that we have.

What we trust in, we are devoted to; what we are devoted to, we put our trust in. The story of David and Goliath may be the most well-known Biblical account. It was David's first battle. He entered it armed with a sling and five smooth stones. Because the young man trusted in the Lord, only one stone was necessary for the giant to come tumbling down.

That experience set King David up for more battles. Every combat engagement required the same decision: trust in the Lord or man-made weaponry. In Psalm 20:7 we read where his devotion lay, "Some trust in chariots and some in horses, but we trust in the name of the Lord our God."

We may not be in a literal battle, but many things contend for our devotion: Bitcoin and bank accounts, the stock market and savings accounts, property and pensions, reputation and recreation, talents and treasures.

Loving Jesus most protects us from all kinds of evil. For those who say *money is the root of all evil*, they are wrong. For the one who believes *the love of money is the root of all evil*, they too, are incorrect.

So that our devotion has the proper direction, the truth needs to be retaught. 1 Timothy 6:10 speaks the truth, "For the love of money is a root of all kinds of evil…" Like David's small stone, it is the little words that pack the punch.

The one-lettered word, *a*. Did you catch it? Look again! The love of money is not *the* root of all evil it is *a* root of *all kinds* of evil. Now that it has been taught, was it also caught? Until it is, when it comes to our treasures, we cannot serve the Lord with our whole hearts.

KEY THOUGHT TO DAILY STAND: What vies for your devotion and attempts to master you?

Day 14

Affliction

KEY VERSE: *If they obey and serve him, they will spend the rest of their days in prosperity and their years in contentment. Job 36:11*

Job knew affliction.

The Bible says, with God's permission, Satan attacked Job. A messenger escaped to report the first of four back-to-back tragedies. First, after the Sabeans killed all the servants by the sword then they carried off Job's oxen and donkeys. Second, before that report was finished, another messenger came and told of lightning that burned up Job's sheep and killed more servants. Third, before he was done speaking, a third messenger reported the Chaldeans raided Job's camels, carried them off, and took the servants down by the sword.

Fourth, as if that was not enough for one man to bear and difficult to grasp, another messenger delivered the worst news of the day. While all of Job's children—his seven sons and three daughters—were feasting at the oldest brother's house, a mighty wind hit the house and it collapsed. Job lost all his children.

Throughout the trauma, Job did not sin. He was broken up, but not broken. He was pressured to fall apart, but he chose to praise God (Job 1:21).

Neglecting to serve the Lord has no excuse—including through affliction. In Job 36, Elihu continues a speech to Job. In Job 36:8, he mentions people who are bound and shackled by the cords of distress from the sin in their life. In Job 36:9, he says God uses affliction to get their attention for correction that leads to repentance.

Yes, Job was acquainted with grief. Let us not forget, so was Jesus.

Isaiah 53:3 prophesied about our Savior, "He was despised and rejected by men, a man of sorrows, and familiar with suffering."

In his daily devotional on June 23, Oswald Chambers writes, "We are not a*cquainted with grief* in the same way our Lord was acquainted with it. We endure it and live through it, but we do not become intimate with it." We experience deep, gut-wrenching pain from our personal tragedies, but Jesus bore the weight of all sin—all of the sin, of all of humanity, for all time.

I met a man who told of how he fell into a pit of sin. As a pastor he embezzled money from his church and was addicted to drugs. He told me, "It wasn't until I was so bound up in my sin that God finally had my attention."

Years have passed, his recovery intact, but he is awaiting his prison sentence for the crimes he committed. The shackles he will soon wear will serve as a consequence of his sin. Though his hands will be cuffed, his heart has been set free. Though his home will be a prison cell, his mind and soul will live joyfully.

God used his affliction to get his attention. Now the man knows redemption and reconciliation with his Savior. He is ready to serve the Lord in and out of chains.

KEY QUESTION TO DAILY STAND: How has God used affliction to get your attention?

Day 15

Fervor Fever

KEY VERSE: *Never be lacking in zeal, but keep your spiritual fervor, serving the Lord. Romans 12:11*

    A certain commercial for Geico Insurance cracks me up. A sloth is playing Pictionary. The people playing with the sloth are guessing what he is drawing. After twenty-five seconds time is up and the people have made eleven incorrect guesses from the two-inch straight line drawn by the sloth.

    The sloth commercial is fun but other versions of Romans 12:11 begin, "Do not be slothful…" It is to be unwilling, unambitious, disinterested—to have a reluctant attitude. It can also describe idleness, laziness, and timidity. These traits are inadequate and unsuitable for serving the Lord.

    Zeal is the real deal. Romans 12:1 begins, "Never lacking in zeal…" The original word is speedy diligence. It means to quickly obey what the Lord reveals. What we think is good enough, zeal will reveal what is better or more important.

    So that we do not lack in zeal, the solution is to keep our spiritual fervor. The King James Version says, "…fervent in spirit…" The word fervent is used twice in the New Testament.

    Acts 18:25 describes Apollos. "…he spoke with great fervor and spoke about Jesus accurately…" That would be a remarkable epitaph to have inscribed on a grave marker. Oh, to leave a legacy like that! To be known for having had a zealous walk of faith!

    What is spiritual fervor? It means hot enough to boil. Figuratively, it is to inwardly boil with interest or desire. All followers of Jesus should be identified as zealous and exhibiting a fervent fever. Our hearts should burn with passion and zeal for Jesus. We ought to serve the Lord from the overflow of our deep commitment to Him. Our service to Him should burn bright and illuminate the darkness in the world around us.

Too often we comment on how we need to grow in our relationship with the Lord. At times we complain that we are stuck on our faith journey. What zapped the zeal? What doused the desire?

How do we keep our spiritual fervor from lacking zeal? Romans 12:11 has the solution. "…serving the Lord."

KEY THOUGHT TO DAILY STAND: If your epitaph matched your zeal and fervor, what would it say?

Day 16

Take Heed

KEY VERSE: *Be careful, or you will be enticed to turn away and serve other gods and bow down to them. Deuteronomy 11:16*

If my three-year-old granddaughter was getting too close to the three steps off my deck, I would gently tell her, "Be careful, Sweetie, you're close to the edge and you don't want to fall."

However, if I was home last fall when my husband was at the top of the ladder, and I noticed that it was hung up at the edge of our house, I could have hollered a warning to him, "Babe! Watch out! The ladder is unsteady!"

No one was present when the extension ladder got hung up on the roof. In seconds the extension locks unhooked, descending the ladder, flipping my husband backward, and catching his leg between two rungs. Unfortunately, he landed on his head in an upside-down, yet lopsided heap in the yard. He definitely could have used a *take heed*!

Take heed! There are times on our faith journey we get close to the edge of a slight spiritual decline. Then there are other times we think we are steadily walking by faith, but something has us hung up and we are unaware of the pending spiritual downfall.

A gentle *be careful* is not an appropriate warning for a spiritual misstep. We need a *take heed*! Although some versions of Deuteronomy 11:16 begin with, "Be careful…," it is not meant to be gentle; rather, it is to give careful attention *to beware* to guard and preserve and protect.

Today's theme verse ends with a consequence, begins with a warning, and sandwiched in between, is what gets us hung up, no longer walking by faith.

Enticement.

Defined, *entice* is to be led on by exciting hope or desire, to be allured and deceived. Enticement was the first encounter between Satan and humanity. The serpent enticed Adam and Eve with a lie, and they were deceived to believe the enticer over their Lord. Proof that we need to take heed! God gives the warning, but much like something that is taught must be caught, a warning must be heeded so we are spiritually guarded, preserved, and protected.

Worshiping other gods is irreverent; yet sadly, it is commonplace amongst Christians. Anything that we set our affection and devotion on more than Jesus is a god. Take heed!

Children, grandchildren, husband, wife, career, reputation, ministry, possessions, pride, ability, talent—if you are hung up on them or more devoted to them more than you are to Jesus, they are a god. Take heed!

We declare through hymn and song, "I need Thee every hour," and "Lord, I need you, oh, I need you." Are the words just coming off your lips or are they the cry of your heart?

We are free to live as we please. But the choices we make come with a cost. Take heed! Enticement will lead us away from Jesus and the downfall will have us bowing down to things we never intended.

The warning is set. Take heed!

KEY SUGGESTION TO DAILY STAND: Today, be careful and on guard against enticement.

Day 17

Listen Up!

KEY VERSE: *…fear the Lord, serve him, obey his voice...*1 Samuel 12:14

The Voice is a televised singing competition. Admittedly, I like it, but not for the celebrity status. I do not get starry-eyed or giddy over the famous or the renowned. I like the story behind the contestants and watching raw talent blossom. But that is not the point.

The first round is my favorite. They call it the blind auditions. Contestants sing on a stage as the four judges are turned around with their back to the singers. Contenders are chosen solely on their voice. Normally our first impression of a person is what they look like, not what they sound like.

Is this true of your experience with God? What has your attention? What He looks like or what He sounds like—His character or His voice? Most Christians can readily name the traits of God. He is faithful, trustworthy, good, gracious, merciful, helpful, loving, kind, forgiving, and more! But they are reticent to describe His voice.

According to 1 Samuel 12:24, God's children should fear Him, serve Him, and obey His voice. How can we obey a voice we cannot describe? If we are unfamiliar with His voice, how will we know when He is speaking to us?

Both great questions. First, God's Word is His voice. As you read the Bible, imagine God speaking the words right to you. Next, a moral compass and code are built within every person. Since we are created in the image of God, His character can be ours. Finally, when we become aware of wrongdoing, it is not because we are smart and wise; rather, it is the voice of God, through His Spirit, revealing the sin and the way of correction.

Some people struggle with God as their Father

because they filter Him through their earthly parent. To hear the voice of God properly and productively, this must be corrected. God created you; therefore, He first saw you, knew you, and loved you. And because He never changes, He still sees you, knows you, and loves you.

One day I raised my voice in correction to my then eight-year-old boy. He inquired, "Momma, why are you yelling?" At the top of my lungs, I responded, "*This* is yelling. You tell me, son, was I previously yelling or just raising my voice?" He got the point.

God speaks in a still small voice, and at times He thunderously bellows. I once heard a preacher say, "I think God speaks in a whisper so we will lean in to hear Him." If we interpret His still, small voice as God only whispering sweet things to us, then we are misinformed. A well-placed whisper can be a bellow of correction from the Lord. After all, God loves those He corrects and disciplines (Proverbs 3:11-12).

To serve the Lord, we must also obey Him; we must listen to His voice. While you are waiting for a whisper from God, pick up your Bible and read it. His Word speaks loud and clear.

KEY THOUGHT TO DAILY STAND: Stop talking and listen for the voice of God.

Day 18

Conjunction Connection

KEY VERSE: *...and serve him shoulder to shoulder...Zephaniah 3:9*

From 1973 to 1984 School House Rock creatively taught children the basics of grammar and other important subjects. The animated short films were played during the Saturday-morning cartoon lineup. The popularity continued off the airwaves as schoolteachers still use them in the classroom.

One of the top catchy tunes is "Conjunction Junction." The song asks the question, "What is the function of a conjunction?" Then answers, "Hooking up words and phrases and clauses."

In the middle of Zephaniah 3:9 sits a conjunction. If all we did was focus on the latter half of today's key verse, we would miss the vital connection. "Then I will purify the lips of the peoples, that all of them may call on the name of the Lord and serve him shoulder to shoulder."

God used the prophet Zephaniah to warn the people of Judah that their desertion and departure from God would bring them pending doom. But Zephaniah also declared restoration and redemption would come by way of a remnant of faithful followers.

The imagery of serving the Lord shoulder to shoulder is quite attractive and appealing.

Prior to the verse Zephaniah is prophesying about the judgment of the Lord. The first word of Zephaniah 3:9 indicates a shift in theme. Redemption is now the focus. Should the people wake up and listen to the rebuke, and observe God's correction, *then…*

2 Timothy 3:16 is for those who read God's Word, who listen and obey. "All Scripture is God-breathed and is

useful..." It is profitable and valuable; advantageous for, "...teaching, rebuking, correcting, and training up in righteousness."

Zephaniah continued speaking to the people who were paying attention and believed the message, "Then will I purify the lips of the peoples, that all of them may call on the name of the Lord..." (Zephaniah 3:9a).

Jesus said, "For the mouth speaks what the heart is full of" (Luke 6:45, Good News Translation). Pure hearts speak with clean lips. Clean hearts call on the name of the Lord.

Zephaniah 3:17 says, "The Lord your God is with you, he is mighty to save. He will take delight in you, he will quiet you with his love, he will rejoice over you with singing." As followers of Jesus we must be careful we do not disconnect the promises of God from the judgment of God.

This promise is for, "...the meek and humble who trust in the name of the Lord...the remnant...will speak no lies, nor will deceit be found in their mouths..." (Zephaniah 3:12-13).

And.

Standing clean before the Lord allows us to serve Him should-to-shoulder, alongside our brothers and sisters in Christ.

Redemption restores relationship.

Recently, Russia invaded and initiated war with Ukraine. As I write this my husband is in Hungary, serving the Lord on a short-term mission opportunity. Kevin is shoulder to shoulder with his team, delivering medical and food supplies just over the Ukrainian border.

Before you stand shoulder to shoulder to serve the Lord, use portions of Psalm 24 as your personal plea. *Lord, give me 'clean hands and a pure heart' as I seek You and Your face. Thank you, for Your strength and might. I choose to serve You wholly and rightly.*

KEY THOUGHT TO DAILY STAND: The promises of God are conditional on our obedience.

The longer I serve Him,
the sweeter He grows,
The more that I love Him,
more love He bestows;
Each day is like heaven,
my heart overflows,
The longer I serve Him,
the sweeter He grows.

"The Longer I Serve Him"
By: Bill Gaither

Day 19

The Sin Factor

KEY VERSE: *…we should not serve sin… Romans 6:6*

It is imperative that followers of Jesus know their base power and are sure of their faith foundation. We all yield to, submit to, obey, and serve something that is not part of our faith foundation. And whatever that something is, we are enslaved to it.

Christians must use godly wisdom and respond righteously to cultural demands of division and alienation from ideologies. In many versions of the Bible, Romans 6:6 ends, "…we should no longer be slaves to sin."

A popular worship song declares, "I'm no longer a slave to fear." We confidently sing the word slave, but we are timid to speak about it.

In his letter to the Romans, Paul uses terminology all persons would understand—then and now.

Let us first focus on sin. Paul writes a great deal about the topic because sin is a huge deal in our lives. Romans 6:6 begins, "For we know that our old self was crucified…"

We need to stop here. *For we know* draws a conclusion and assumption. Before we can accept the end of this verse, we need to acknowledge that our old self is no more.

For we know our old self was crucified, right? Then, why do we accept *sinner* as an identity marker? Jesus saves us from the penalty of sin; He also saves us from the power of sin, but until we are called home to glory, we remain in the presence of sin. I am not sure who to credit, but *though sin no longer reigns, it still remains* communicates proper position. Before Jesus, sin enslaved me; being in Christ, He is master.

Therefore, Romans 6:6 concludes, "…that we should no longer be slaves to sin." Paul does not say we will never sin again, he states sin no longer controls us, and so we should not serve sin.

When we refer to and announce our status as sinner, perhaps we could see it as conviction. Maybe the Holy Spirit is revealing a link in a sin chain that needs to be broken.

2 Corinthians 5:17 emphatically states, "If anyone is in Christ, they are a new creation; the old has gone, the new has come."

It is time followers of Jesus live as He intends—no longer slaves to sin!

KEY CHALLENGE TO DAILY STAND: If we are in Christ, let us live like it!

Day 20

Commitment

KEY VERSE: *...commit yourselves to the Lord and serve him only...1 Samuel 7:3*

As we raised our six kids, Kevin and I taught them that their word mattered. If they promised something, it was expected they keep it. If they made a commitment, they would see it through to the end, no shortcuts or bailing allowed.

Commitment is a part of integrity. For Christians commitment is a matter of the heart. I realize some divorces are necessary and called for, but I also know people who abandoned marriage for less than what Kevin and I have fought over throughout our 34 years of covenant together.

When it comes to our walk with Jesus, commitment is crucial. Too many followers of Jesus settle at salvation, remaining in shallow waters. They choose sink over swim in matters of maturity. God calls us to go deep. Deeper in devotion and deeper in duty.

Let us narrow commitment to three parts. Spake. Take. Make.

Spake. Making a commitment to the Lord requires words and action. First, a word of promise to be devoted to Him, to serve Him, love Him, observe His commands, and walk in all His ways. Next, a vow to renounce the former things that once brought happiness, gratification, and satisfaction.

We cannot truly serve the Lord until we renounce and rid ourselves of past pleasures and ungodly loyalties. Historical Biblical commentator Matthew Henry, who died in 1714, said, "True repentance strikes at the darling sin...the sin that most easily besets us." Absolute and wholehearted service to the Lord, calls for total abandonment of idols and ideologies that do not align with His Word and His ways.

Take. Take your commitment to the Lord seriously. Say what you mean and mean what you say and do what you mean. Spiritual integrity is righteousness. Right living is a lifestyle modeled after God's statutes. Know that hardship is part of commitment, so commit now to stay the course. Be aware storms will assail, trouble will assault, and people may attack your devotion and dedication. Remember, you are committed to serving the Lord and He is your rock and refuge, your safety and shelter.

Make. Make a commitment to make it last. Serving the Lord pleases the Lord. Oh, that we would live a life pleasing to Him before we live waiting for Him to appease us. True and lasting commitment stays the course and trusts the Lord. When we stay we will not stray.

KEY QUESTION TO DAILY STAND: Along your faith journey, what spiritual commitment needs to be shored up or strengthened?

Day 21

If…Then.

KEY VERSE: *…if you faithfully obey the commands…to love the Lord your God and to serve him with all your heart and with all your soul—then…Deuteronomy 11:13-14*

I had the privilege of being raised in a good neighborhood. There were a few girls my age, which made this extroverted child very content. One day Debbie wanted our group to come to play in her backyard. She had a stipulation. If we ate a dog treat, then we gained entrance.

If was the condition, *then* was the assurance.

In Deuteronomy 10:12-13, Moses laid out the SLOW living plan. Serve God, Love God, Observe His commands, and Walk in all His ways. And in Deuteronomy 11:13-15, Moses asserts a condition to the Israelites, followed by an assurance, as they wandered in the wilderness.

Condition: "If you faithfully obey the commands I am giving you today—to love the Lord your God and to serve him with all your heart and with all your soul…" (Deuteronomy 11:13).

Assurance: "…then I will send rain…I will provide grass…and you will eat and be satisfied" (Deuteronomy 11:14-15).

We cannot wander well through the wilderness if we want the assurance before we are willing to meet the condition. And yet, how many times do we pray for the things we need and plead for the things of God, expecting they will bring us satisfaction? Meanwhile, we are serving *our* needs, loving *our* ways, observing *our* standards, and walking where *we* want, ignoring the *if* as we anticipate the *then*.

It is audacious and foolish to expect the Lord, God Almighty, Maker of Heaven and Earth, to overlook and excuse His conditions so we can receive His provision and protection without participation in the stipulations.

The next time we are in a spiritual famine, before we pray for rain, we ought to have a self-examination and check for conditional neglect on our part.

If it is not well with our soul, before we seek to be satisfied, we should seek to faithfully obey the Lord—to love and serve Him with all our heart and with all our soul.

God's Word is clear: *If* we faithfully obey the commands he gives, *then* He will send the rain, provide the grass, and we will be satisfied.

KEY QUESTION TO DAILY STAND: What *if* have you neglected because you have been focused on a particular *then* from God?

Day 22

This Pleases God

KEY VERSE: *…anyone who serves Christ in this way is pleasing to God…Romans 14:18*

Is "*Lord, I hope I brought You pleasure today*" included in your bedtime prayers? It is far more common to let God know what He did to gratify and satisfy us. And it is acceptable to let Him know we are pleased with His faithfulness and provision. But when was the last time you considered what pleases God?

Notice what Romans 14:18 does not say: Anyone who serves Christ is pleasing to God. When we remove *in this way*, we tend to dictate the way. Years ago, I heard a quote from Charles Swindoll that became a mainstay on my faith journey. "We must do God's will, God's way."

One of the greatest stumbling blocks and strongholds that trip up followers of Jesus along their faith journey is when we aim to do God's will our way. According to Romans 14:17, if we truly desire to serve Christ to please God, it will be done *in this way*: not concerned with trivial matters.

Romans 14:17 begins, "For the kingdom of God is not a matter of eating and drinking…" In my New International Version Study Bible, the note for this verse says, "To be concerned with such trivial matters is to miss completely the essence of Christian living."

And then Paul continues with three worthy and imperative things that matter to the kingdom of God.

    1. **Righteousness in the Holy Spirit**. After an examination of our soul by God, He deems what is right and gives His approval. Yes, His will must be lived out His way, but

righteousness is also determined by Him. And it comes to us by way of the Holy Spirit who enables and empowers us to live righteously and serve Christ in motivation and action.

2. **Peace in the Holy Spirit**. Do not be deceived, this is not external peace. This is from the inside out. It is peace of mind and tranquility of the soul. It is being assured that because of salvation in Christ, we do not need to fear anything; we are content with whatever our lot, so we declare it is well with our soul. We spend an exorbitant amount of time praying for peace in this world when God is clear that peace only comes through His Son, the Prince of Peace. And when we serve Christ to please God, we exhibit peaceful living in the Holy Spirit.

3. **Joy in the Holy Spirit**. Do not confuse this with happiness. This is deep-rooted gladness with its source centered only in Christ. I say it often, but I have never prayed for my kids to be happy, nor will I ever. Do I want them happy? Of course. However, it is my heart's prayer they will know true and lasting joy through all celebration, but more so in suffering, as they serve Christ and please God. But more, I desire they personally know Jesus and the power of His resurrection, and that they choose to live exclusively for Him, serving and loving God with their whole hearts.

KEY POINT TO DAILY STAND: God's will must be

done God's way.

O serve the Lord with gladness,
And come before His throne;
He is our great Redeemer,
And He is God alone.

"O Serve the Lord with Gladness"
By: Fanny J. Crosby

Day 23

Turn Around

KEY VERSE: *...They tell how you turned to God from idols to serve the living and true God...1 Thessalonians 1:9*

To me, the song *The Hokey-Pokey* deserves an eyeroll, but I am always amazed as the first few bars of the simple tune are played at a wedding how many guests jump at the opportunity to turn themselves about.

Spiritually, we cannot turn our lives around without the intervening power of God's Spirit to convince us we need a Savior or woo us into a relationship with Him or convict us of sin or turn ourselves around after we abandoned or avoided God's path of righteousness.

Like the prodigal son in Luke 15:17, at some point we all need to come to our senses. God wooed him, but the lost son turned himself around and went back to where he belonged. But before he went back, he needed to turn from the idols he had worshiped.

We serve a God of order. When our lives are out of order, we need His guidance and direction. 1 Thessalonians 1:9 instructs us to turn away from idols and turn to and serve the living and true God.

Too many people think they have completely turned to God while maintaining certain lifestyles and choices. I asked a woman in church one day, "How are things with you?" Her eyes filled with tears, so instead of prodding, I simply wrote my number on a card, gave it to her, and let her know I was a safe place to unload should she decide to call. She did.

She told me how she desperately wanted to feel God near, but for years He seemed distant. After listening and inquiring the Holy Spirit nudged me to gently share godly wisdom and truth. She had been a Christian for years, but she was also cohabitating with a man who was not her husband. Contrary to what cultural opinion is, sexual relations outside marriage, between one man and one woman, is unacceptable. Marriage is God's will, and it must be lived out His way.

Moving out was a good decision; it turned her back on the idols she had been serving. But turning back to God requires a separate step of faith. Doing good and obeying some of God's commands do not turn us completely around.

Following Jesus wholeheartedly, follows Him all the way, in full surrender: Turning our lives around to serve God, love Him, observe His commands, and walk in all His ways.

That's what it's all about.

KEY THOUGHT TO DAILY STAND: Whatever has you living contrary to God's Word, turn your back to it and turn back to God.

Day 24

Search and Rescue

KEY VERSE: *...serve him with wholehearted devotion and with a willing mind...1 Chronicles 28:9*

In my Bible this verse is underlined in blue pen and highlighted in yellow. And in the margin, next to this portion of Scripture, I wrote: *Ministry/Life verse Feb. 2000.* Obviously, to me, it has significant meaning.

King David was talking directly to his son, Solomon, in the presence of all the officials of Israel. He announced that Solomon was next in line to the throne and charged his son to follow all the commands of the Lord (1 Chronicles 28:4-8).

My husband and I have six children. He is their dad, but when they were growing up, he was also their pastor. We have always been intentional in keeping those lines in check. Spiritually, blurred boundaries contribute to distorted perspectives.

In our home Kevin was always daddy, but at church he was Pastor Kevin. On Sunday mornings daddy left the house early to go work, but when the children and I stepped into the church building, we greeted the Pastor. We know it was silly for some, but that does not bother us.

As godly parents it was our responsibility to lay a solid spiritual foundation. When our kids misbehaved in the worship service, the pastor kept preaching, and I handled the disciplinary moments (except the two times when the pastor excused himself from the pulpit to confront two of our boys who thought they could get away with mischief.)

Like King David to Solomon, Kevin unreservedly modeled to our children that God is his Lord, and he acknowledges Him and serves Him with wholehearted devotion and with a willing mind (1 Chronicles 28:9a).

The middle portion of 1 Chronicles 28:9 is today's focus. King David continued talking to Solomon, "…for the Lord searches every heart and understands the motive behind the thoughts…"

First, the Lord searches our hearts. He is constantly searching and investigating, even to the deepest parts. The nooks, crannies, closets, and corners are thoroughly examined. Next, He understands every motive behind our thoughts. He perceives and discerns our intellectual framework.

We cannot stop God from searching our souls. However, we have a choice in how we respond. If we are unsettled, intimidated, or apprehensive, a change in perspective is necessary. God loves you. He cares for you. No one will love or care more. His search of your heart is also a rescue operation. If His examination exposes missteps, mishaps, or mistakes then He will also reveal a transformative plan.

When it comes to serving the Lord, motive matters. Are we diligent so we get noticed by what we accomplished? Do we serve to make us feel better about ourselves? Are we let down when we do not receive a thank you from others? If so, we need His rescue.

Or do you serve God because you love Him and desire that Jesus be glorified through all you do? If so, carry on.

KEY POINT TO DAILY STAND: Wholeheartedly serving God requires His search and, if necessary, His rescue plan.

Day 25

Pay Attention to Directions

KEY VERSE: *Do not turn aside from any of the commands I give you today, to the right or to the left, following other gods and serving them…Deuteronomy 28:14*

    I read an article about people who blindly followed their Global Positioning Systems (GPS) and landed in irreversible predicaments. A sedan was driven into the sand on a golf course, a box truck got stuck between trees on a bicycle path, a semi-truck was smashed between brick walls in an alley, and an SUV was floating on a lake near a ferry boat.
    Another story told of a man driving in dense fog. He thought he was at a familiar intersection that would require him to continue straight, but the GPS directed him to turn left. He listened to the computerized voice and drove into a stranger's living room.
    Joshua did not need a GPS. After Moses died God went to Joshua, the leader of His people, and gave him instructions to cross the Jordan River and enter the Promised Land. But first, God made a promise and gave commands. He promised He would never leave, nor forsake, Joshua.
    God encouraged Joshua to be strong and courageous. He cautioned him to be careful to obey His law. And then God commanded, "…do not turn from it to the right or to the left, that you may be successful wherever you go."
    Deuteronomy 28 has two sub-topics: Blessings for Obedience and Curses for Disobedience. The last thing Moses writes before he mentions the curses is, "Do not turn aside from any of the commands…to the right or to the left…" Moses had said this same thing before, but he also told the people to stay on the path and to follow all the

directions the Lord gave them (Deuteronomy 5:32-33).

God orders the steps of His children (Psalm 37:23). But He will not force us to walk them; that is our choice. He is delighted when we stay on His paths.

When we stray it is not happenstance. No! Ignorance or innocence will not have us turn to the right or to the left. It might be hasty or impulsive, but it is deliberate; furthermore, it is negligent and reckless.

Deuteronomy 28:14 concludes with what happens when we turn off God's intended path, whether to the right or to the left. We follow and serve other gods.

And that has grave and grievous consequences. Therefore, do as Joshua was told. "Do not let [God's Word] depart from your mouth; meditate on it day and night, so that you may be careful to do everything written in it" (Joshua 1:8).

KEY CHALLENGE TO DAILY STAND: Memorize Psalm 37:23.

Day 26

Spirit vs. Flesh

KEY VERSE: *…serve the Law of God with my mind, but with my flesh I serve the law of sin. Romans 7:25*

There are five years between my first and fourth child. My first four children were born in the span of five years. I remember sitting on the kitchen floor and hollering, "Would you please just stop!" at the top of my lungs, as my five-year-old stared at me, the four-year-old and two-year-old kept screaming, and the baby inconsolably cried.

That was not the only time when I did what I did not want to do, and what I knew I needed to do I did not do. Paul describes it this way, "I do not understand what I do. For what I want to do I do not do, but what I hate I do" (Romans 7:15).

Welcome to the ever-popular battle between the spirit and the flesh. There is a war in our world, and it is not man against man. It is Spiritual warfare. And it is personal. We have an enemy and his name is Satan. But for those who are in Christ, we have the victory. And yet, because we breathe oxygen, we live in enemy territory.

In Romans 7:25, Paul says in his mind—meaning, by faith, God's thoughts become his thoughts—he serves God. But, in his flesh—meaning, apart from walking by faith—he serves his sinful nature.

To quit sinful patterns we need to be transformed. And according to Romans 12:2, that requires a renewing of our minds: a spiritual change of both heart and life. Our thoughts come from Him, and our desires get aligned with His word.

When we are serving the law of God, we press into Christ and remain attached and abiding to him, The True Vine (John 15:1-8).

- We need the fullness of the Spirit of God to inhabit our minds and occupy our souls.
- We need His power to fight the sin battle that wages.
- We need His presence to comfort us.
- We need His counsel to show us how to properly serve the Lord in reverence.
- We need His conviction when our flesh is feeding our sinful nature.
- We need His revelation to illumine the Word of God so we can delight in God's Law.

And we need His guidance to lead us on paths of righteousness so we can do what we know we ought to do and we do not do what we know we should not do.

KEY POINT TO DAILY STAND: Being saved from sin secures our eternal home. But being filled with the Spirit allows us to live as Jesus intends until we are called home.

Day 27

Proper Fear

KEY VERSE: *Serve the Lord with fear and rejoice with trembling. Psalm 2:11*

    The word choice and placement in this verse are interesting. Would it not make more sense to serve the Lord with joy and tremble with fear? Remember, we serve a God of order who is perfect in all His ways. Therefore, the Psalmist wrote it as God inspired and instructed him.

    What does it mean to rejoice with trembling? First, let us focus on the word rejoice. It means to be glad, to be joyful, and to delight in. This verb is used a total of forty-four times in the Old Testament: nineteen times throughout the Psalms, but it is also used nineteen times by six prophets: Isaiah, Hosea, Joel, Habakkuk, Zechariah, and Zephaniah.

    Prophets were appointed and anointed by God to deliver His message to His people. Generally, prophets reminded the people of God's loving-kindness, His rescue, and provision, but they also warned of God's judgment and the pending consequences should they disobey and disregard His commands.

    Next, trembling. Think shudder. We tend to think of this through fear, horror, or a reaction to being cold. The Bible uses contrasting themes, at times paradoxes, to make a point clear. True honor, respect, and awe in our Lord, ought to compel us to stand in fear before Him.

    Horror and fright are not the right motivators! Devotion and reverence convince us to bow and worship before the Lord. As we stand in awe and wonder of His goodness and mercy, our souls should shudder at His magnificence and majesty, His grandeur and glory.

    His splendor is unreachable, but not unapproachable. His forgiveness of us is undeserving, but He chooses to offer us His amazing grace. His ways are higher than ours, but He shares them with us anyway. His love reaches to the heavens, but envelops humanity, too. His Word never changes but it transforms us; it is sharper than a double-edged sword to pierce our souls but shows us how to truly live. For this, and more, we are compelled to rejoice with trembling.

The Psalmist begins *serve the Lord with fear*. Fear of the Lord is the premise for these daily readings. It is SLOW living. Current Christian culture would have us focus more on the love and acceptance of God. And though these attributes are good and vital to our relationship with Him, they generally do not have us standing in fear before him.

Many people refuse to focus or give any endorsement to the justice part of God—they believe His justice is social, and yet, that is manmade terminology. Yes, we should care for the widows and the orphans, the sick and the needy—we are commanded in God's Word to do so. But what we will not find in His Word is tolerance for what makes others happy and acceptance for the way they choose to live.

Social justice has us serving others first, but we are called to serve the Lord and out of that reverence, we serve others—the way He intends and commands, not the way we want and culture dictates or demands.

Proper fear trembles before the Lord, accepting His will and His ways—that will make us joyful and glad.

KEY QUESTION TO DAILY STAND: Do you see it as your duty to serve the Lord with fear and rejoice with trembling?

Day 28

Thy Will or My Will?

KEY VERSE: *Serve the Lord…he will…Exodus 23:25*

We love to know and experience what God says He will do for us. But it is worth repeating: We serve Him out of love and gratitude for who He is, not for what He does for us. Serving the Lord is a command, yet it is also a choice.

In Exodus 23:20-33, God is informing Moses how He will prepare and pave the way into the Promised Land and how He will purify the land. Throughout these fourteen verses is a smattering of *I wills* and a smidge of *do nots*.

Because He is a good Father, He chooses to enlighten His children about His promises. They are not secret, and nothing is omitted. But if we focus on the *do nots* His *I wills* will still happen. Conversely, if we only center on the *I wills* the *do nots* will still occur.

When we have our eyes on ourselves, we tend to be attracted to the *I wills*, while avoiding the *do nots*. At times we act as if God exists to meet our individual expectations. Another thing worth repeating: Jesus did not come to meet our expectations; He came to meet our need.

Today we will dive into the *do nots* as if their lives depended on them—or, rather, because their lives *were* dependent on them:

- Do not rebel and listen carefully.
- Do all that I say.
- Do not bow to their gods.
- Do not worship their gods.
- Do not follow their practices.
- You must demolish their sacred stones.
- Worship the Lord your God.
- Do not make a covenant with the people of

- the land or with their gods.
- Do not let them live in your land, or they will cause you to sin.

Recently I spoke at a women's retreat in a different denomination from my own. I was conversing with a woman whose husband is in denominational leadership. There is mounting concern over the rigidity of their polity and the sternness of its structure for implementation.

Though I understand and respect the value in evaluation of governance, as the Body of Christ we must be careful and diligent we do not water down or weaken the will of God for His people for the sake of the pursuit of change. In a desire to be contemporary, godly wisdom is essential. Changing verbiage must not change His Word. Changing strategies cannot change His will.

The *I wills* outnumber the *do nots*. Depending on the version used and counting the *I have*, *I am*, and *will be's*, there are about twenty—twice as many promises as commands. He truly is a good God. That should not be our reason to serve, but it does prove we cannot outgive Him or love our faithful Father more than He loves us.

KEY CHALLENGE TO DAILY STAND: Notice all the good things God brings your way today, then consider how you will or did serve Him in this day.

Day 29

Would You Rather…?

KEY VERSE: *…rather, serve one another in love. Galatians 5:13*

Perhaps you have played the game, *Would You Rather*. Dilemmas are read aloud from cards, along with two options for what the player would rather do if they were in the dilemma. Here are some examples:

- Would you rather go into the past and meet your ancestors or go into the future and meet your great-great-grandchildren?
- Would you rather have more time or more money?
- Would you rather be able to talk with the animals or speak all foreign languages?
- Would you rather have a rewind button or a pause button on your life?

There is only one time in history when the sun stood still. Joshua 10:13 tells us, "The sun stopped in the middle of the sky and delayed going down about a full day." Time was paused, but a battle raged on—life went on for God's people.

In Galatians 5, Paul writes to Christians about the freedom we have in Christ. But he cautions we need to be sure we do not take it for granted and use it to indulge our sinful nature. Paraphrasing, there is a *would you rather* for us to consider. Would you rather use your freedom to indulge in sin or use your freedom to serve one another in love?

Paul concludes this portion of the chapter with, "If you keep on biting and devouring each other, watch out or you will be destroyed by each other" (Galatians 5:15). Sandwiched in between the *would you rather* and the warning is a single command that will make us choose wisely and help us serve God as we serve others.

Before I was married I was in church ministry, and with my husband a pastor for twenty-six years, I have been a part of ten different churches. I also have experience in many parachurch organizations. That is a lot of front-row seats for watching how people use the freedom they have in Christ. I would much rather be a part of a Body that loves Jesus most and serves others well, than a church that loves its reputation most and calls its outreach serving.

I have witnessed people get invited in to help, but when they show up, they are not welcomed into the fold. I have been the recipient of *that'll never work* when I expressed a new idea. I have been yelled at, ridiculed, left out, falsely accused, slandered, and more. Though it is not justifiable in most situations, I understand why people leave churches. Frankly, I would rather see the ones who stay, leave—some say, it could be a blessed subtraction.

We cannot change people's souls, that lie solely on the Spirit of God. But we are challenged to live out our freedom one way or the other: indulging in sin or serving one another. It is the single command sandwiched in the verse that makes us choose wisely and helps us serve God.

"Love your neighbor as yourself" (Galatians 5:14). Connecting this command with the consequences mentioned of what happens when we backbite and injure-to-ruin one another, it can be concluded there just might be some self-hate in the church pews.

KEY POINT TO DAILY STAND: Feeding the flesh (the sinful nature), cannot help us love or allow us to serve another.

Day 30

Good News

KEY VERSE: *…he has served with me in the work of the gospel. Philippians 2:22*

    The gospel of Jesus is good news. The angel told the shepherds, "I bring you good news of great joy" (Luke 2:10). The Greek word for good news in this proclamation means gospel—it was the announcement that the Savior of the world had been born.

    However, the Greek word for gospel in Philippians 2:22 is not just limited to the news of salvation. It means God's complete good news that includes the whole of Scripture. Timothy proved he was a faithful and fully devoted follower of Jesus. Paul highlights Timothy as serving in the work of the gospel. What a declaration to have spoken over you!

    Many Christians and ministry leaders serve the Lord in the name of Jesus. They work tirelessly to meet the needs of people, proclaim truth, teach, preach, build buildings, oversee projects and events, visit the sick, comfort the grieving, administer over finances, and more.

    Problems and issues occur in the Body of Christ when self-care overrides and overturns soul-care. If we depose and dethrone the King of kings, we will stop serving people and begin serving ourselves. With eyes on self our egos get fed; we hunger for power, and we become prideful volunteers and leaders.

    According to Paul, Timothy was a solid and trusted servant leader:

- He took a genuine interest in the welfare of the church in Philippi (Philippians 2:20).
- Rather than looking to his own interests, he

- focused on the things of Jesus (Philippians 2:21).
  - And it was all proven as he served in the work of the gospel (Philippians 2:22).

Matthew Henry said, "Seeking our own interest to the neglect of Jesus Christ is a very great sin, and very common among Christians and ministers. Many prefer their own credit, ease, and safety, before truth, holiness, and duty, the things of their own pleasure and reputation before the things of Christ's kingdom and his honor and interest in the world: but Timothy was none of these."

Mr. Henry's first assertion is staggering. It should have our attention. Self-centeredness requires self-examination. "Examine yourselves to see whether you are in the faith…" (2 Corinthians 13:5). Examine means to make proof of. Go ahead. Test your motivation, faithfulness, and devotion. This verse goes on to say if you fail the test, it is because Jesus Christ is not in you—for some, this may mean you are not saved; for Christians, it means somewhere along the way *self* overtook the throne.

Serving the Lord cannot simultaneously serve self. There is only room for one king on the throne of our soul. Ponder and respond to these self-examination questions:

- Who is the king of your life?
- Whom do you serve?
- Why do you serve?
- Are you faithfully serving?
- What are your motivations for serving?
- Has there been a recent substitute for your devotion?
- Are you in negotiations with the Lord regarding service in His name?
- What needs to be rearranged so you can fear the Lord and fully serve Him?

KEY CHALLENGE TO DAILY STAND: Will you serve the Lord in the whole work of the gospel?

BOOK 2
STAND daily
Loving God

"And now, O Israel, what does the Lord require of you but to fear the Lord...to love God..."
Deuteronomy 10:12-13

    Throughout the next thirty days each daily reading will focus on a Scripture with the word *love* in it. Since there was more than one word used that means *love*, if the word is from the Old Testament, it will be the same original word from the Hebrew language. Likewise, if it is from the New Testament, the same Greek word to mean *love* is used.
    Each day's reading is set up in the same manner:

- Title
- Key Verse
- Key Content
- Key Point

    These daily readings are designed to encourage you to grow, challenge you to change, and influence you to live as Jesus intends:

SLOW

Day 1

Wear and Bear the Name

KEY VERSE: *…to love the name of the Lord... Isaiah 56:6*

Though I like my husband's name, it is not why I love him. We are in a covenant with each other. I vowed to God I would love, honor, and cherish Kevin J Harbin until death parts us. Therefore, since September 24, 1988, I wear and bear his name, and we raised our children to understand our family name matters.

When God added four biological children to our family, we chose their first and middle names. Because our two adopted children were six and seven when He brought them home, their first names were intact, but we chose new middle names. However, we all shared the name Harbin.

Followers of Jesus are in the family of God. We all wear His name. But we also bear the name of the Lord. We talk a great deal about loving God—it is the concentration in this daily series for the next thirty days. Loving God wears and bears His name. We must personally ponder—do I wear and bear it well?

Where-are-they-now articles and reports reveal many children of notorious criminals prefer to avoid the spotlight and even change their names. It makes sense. They want to disassociate from the dishonor and detach from the disgrace their parent made of their name.

Perhaps this warrants further challenge and reflection.

- Do I love the name of the Lord?
- Why do I love the name of the Lord?
- How do I bear His name?

- Where am I willing and where do I neglect to wear His name?

Our God is a good Father, and it is our privilege to bring honor to His name. Free-will allows choice. No one forced us into the family of God. To be clear, the Spirit of God pursues and woos, but we choose to enter the relationship made available through His Son. Once we are in the family, we are called His children.

In Isaiah 56:5 God says, "…I will give them an everlasting name that will not be cut off." Praise God! He chooses us forever! So, what can we do to honor that? He does not leave us in the dark. Within Isaiah 56:1-6 God gives His orders. Yes, they are commands, and though we have a choice to obey, His love for us should compel us to comply:

- Do what is right.
- Hold to righteousness.
- Keep the Sabbath.
- Keep hands from doing evil.
- Bind ourselves to the Lord.
- Serve Him.
- Worship Him.
- Hold fast to covenant.

And positioned in the middle of the list, is *to love the name of the Lord*.

KEY POINT TO DAILY STAND: If you are tucked in tight to Jesus, you will wear and bear His name well.

Day 2

Lovingkindness

KEY VERSE: *...steadfast love to them that love me...Exodus 20:6*

It is unclear who to credit for stating that the Ten Commandments are not the Ten Suggestions. But it is very clear in current culture that there are many confused Christians who live like they do not know the difference.

The Word of God is revealed by the Spirit of God. As we read it on our own, we discover nothing. As we encounter tidbits and treasures, clarity and consideration, interpretation and insight, they come by way of revelation, not education. If we view the *dos and do-nots* of Scripture as irritation, repression, or suppression, we will miss the intention of the God we are called to love.

One of the most profound attributes of God is mentioned in the key verse for today. Other versions say mercy, steadfast love, faithful love, kindness, and unfailing love. In the original text, lovingkindness is the Hebrew word *checed*. In this context it is the kindness of God to a great extent; it is the greatness of His mercy.

This past January Kevin and I went to Mexico, exchanging subzero temperatures in northern Michigan for warmth and outdoor enjoyment. One day we were laying poolside with an ocean view, and I looked at Kevin and asked, "What could be better than this?"

We tend to ask the same thing when life is going well, as we experience trouble-free living. The Psalmist declares to the Lord, "Your love is better than life" (Psalm 63:3). However, the Psalmist was not dwelling on Easy Street; he was in a time of intense need. He longs for the security and safety of God's love promised in our covenant with the Lord.

It is easy to praise and love God when life is good. But the command to love God is not contingent on ease or found in easy living. His lovingkindness is modeled for us throughout the Old Testament. In fact, as Moses was receiving the Ten Commandments from the Lord, He promised His lovingkindness—to a thousand generations for those who would love Him and keep His commands (Exodus 20:6).

Covenant love will not be forgotten by the Lord, but it will break from disobedience and unfaithfulness on our part. We must remain committed to His commands. Contrary to popular opinion, it is expected, not suggested, that we faithfully live them out.

If we fear God, we love God. If we say we love Him but do not fear Him, then we are not protected by the terms of His covenant. A deep love for our Lord keeps us steady and focused, living as Jesus intends—in covenant with the Lord and recipients of His lovingkindness.

KEY QUESTION TO DAILY STAND: What command of God have you turned into a suggestion?

Day 3

All-In

KEY VERSION: *Love the Lord your God with all your heart and with all your soul and with all your mind and with all your strength. Mark 12:30*

For more than 50 years *all Laundry Detergent* has been on the market. Their website claims *all POWERFUL all stainlifter detergents are the champions of stain removal.* The marketing angle stresses, "You are the all-capable, all-confident 'all-family,' and we are your detergent."

The Bible uses the word all to make assertions as well. A covenant relationship is all-in. True and lasting love is all-in. Romans 5:8 is one proof of God's love for humanity. "But God demonstrates his own love for us in this: While we were still sinners, Christ died for us."

Perhaps the most well-known Scripture is John 3:16. It begins, "For God so loved…" It infers an I-love-you-plus! God is all-in with His love for us. It restores! It redeems! It revives! It is complete! It never fails!

We are called to love God with 100% of our heart, soul, mind, and strength. Since 100% concludes and implies excellence, even perfection, is it necessary to use percentages over 100? When someone says, "I am 120% sure," I wonder, if I claim, "I am 100% sure," what makes their assuredness surer than mine? All-in in love is not a number, but you can be sure, it is complete and whole.

God is infinite and eternal; therefore, His love will always be an I-love-you-plus. One of the amazing things about God's everlasting love is it has no end. It is hard to wrap our feeble brains around His never-ending love, but we crave it and we rely on it to teach us how to love Him back and keep us in His love.

Being in Christ secures us for eternal life with Jesus.

But until our graduation to glory, Jesus says the greatest and most important command is to be all-in as we love the Lord:

- With all your heart—to the core of who we are
- With all your soul—our distinct personality
- With all your mind—critical thinking/thorough reasoning
- With all your strength—a force to overcome immediate resistance

Let us listen and do all of what this most important commandment says!

KEY POINT TO DAILY STAND: To be all-in, we must surrender all.

Day 4

Salvation Ovation

KEY VERSE: *…may all who seek you rejoice and be glad in you; may those who love your salvation always say, 'The Lord be exalted'…Psalm 40:16*

Thanksgiving is a time to be grateful for the bounty and harvest throughout the year. A couple of years ago, weeks before the November holiday, my husband and I unexpectedly lost our jobs. And because Kevin's compensation included housing, we lost a place to live, as well. But a paycheck and roof over our heads are not the only bounties we should be grateful for.

Kevin and I gained much when we lost much. A harvest happened in our souls when we recognized the bounty God provided in that wilderness. We were challenged to look closely and dig deep for the ways God showed up and showed off in our time of need.

As followers of Jesus, we should back the train up to where our journey with Jesus began, especially if we have been walking with Him for a long time. Looking back to the time and place of our salvation is good food for our souls.

I was eight years old when I knelt at an altar, placed my bony elbows on the rail, folded my small hands, and invited Jesus into my heart. On that warm July day in 1972, salvation was mine! My life was saved; my slate was wiped clean. I became a follower of Jesus, and I knew my eternal home was secured.

Though I gave my heart to Jesus, it took many years before I accepted the fullness of God and yielded my entire soul to His control. I refer to that first step of faith as the moment I knew Jesus as my Savior. When I turned 30 years old, I accepted Him as my Lord.

Loving God loves His salvation. As I sit at my desk

writing this, I am overwhelmed with gratitude, tears are pooling in my eyes, as I look back with my mind's eye to recall that spunky, blonde girl jumping up from the wooden pew then walking down the aisle to the altar in that outdoor tabernacle at the summer camp where salvation came to little Ellen Schweizer. Today I love God that He reminds me and calls me to love my salvation.

But wait! There is more!

Thankfulness and gratitude for our salvation require a response. Together, we are to *always* exclaim, "The Lord be exalted!" It means to go on without interruption. No matter what enters our lives; no matter the distraction or trouble or crisis; whether pain through loss or heartache, we should be mindful to *always* exalt the Lord *because* we love our salvation.

KEY SUGGESTION TO DAILY STAND: Go throughout your day remembering the joy of your salvation!

Day 5

No Space

KEY VERSE: *…the Lord set his affections on your forefathers and loved them, and he chose you…Deuteronomy 10:15*

    The words of Moses in Deuteronomy were for the Israelite people. The covenant renewal was given to prepare them to exit the wilderness and enter the Promised Land. Renewal can include reminders. Their forefathers were the forerunners of the covenant God established. Abraham was the first man in their ancestry who God called into this special relationship. Isaac and Jacob followed him. And then Jacob had 12 sons.
    When the Israelites entered Egypt, there were 70 Hebrew people. For over 400 years, they remained in bondage, but God allowed them to be fruitful and they multiplied. When Moses led them out of Egypt and they landed in the wilderness, estimations have them over one million people. Moses said their count was, "…as numerous as the stars in the sky" (Deuteronomy 10:22). It was to that massive crowd, Moses gave a reminder that the Lord set His affections on their ancestors, and He loved them.
    God chose to attach His love to them. He made it so that they would tuck in tight to Him, with no space between His heart and theirs. When we attach to God through his covenant of love, there is no space for any other loyalty, devotion, or adoration.
    We will never be removed from His affection, but when disloyalty, unfaithfulness, and disregard carry us away, our souls will detach and turn us away from Him.
We need reminders; we need renewal.
    The Israelites were God's chosen people. Not only were they reminded of God's love, but their hearts would

also be renewed as they were reminded that He chose them. Moses said, "...[God] loved them and he chose you..." (Deuteronomy 10:15).

Earlier in his speech, Moses said, "The Lord your God has chosen you out of all the peoples on the face of the earth to be his people, his treasured possession" (Deuteronomy 7:6).

God is omniscient, sovereign, and judicious. He is perfect in all His ways (Psalm 18:30). He made them His divine choice. When God made His covenant with Abraham and later confirmed it, that began an eternal attachment and holy connection. Jesus came through this very bloodline; He was born to die so we could be eternally attached and personally know this holy connection. God chose this way for us to be in covenant with Him.

Portions of Ephesians 1:4-5 say, "He chose us...before the creation of the world...in love...he [marked out beforehand] to adopt us..." Through Jesus, He sets His affections on us, He loves us, He chose to be in a relationship with us, and He set a plan for it to happen.

Take note!

- He chose you—before the foundation of the world.
- He chose you—in love.
- He chose to adopt you—He set that plan in motion.

What is your response to that?

KEY POINT TO DAILY STAND: Accepting God's covenant of love accepts the terms.

Day 6

Obedience Weighs Nothing

KEY VERSE: *This is love for God…1 John 5:3*

Have you been present when someone receives a gift, but instead of revealing the contents, leaves everyone in suspense? And when the recipient exclaims, "*This is* fabulous! You didn't need to—*this is* too generous! I'm overwhelmed, *this is* just too much!" Everyone is wondering what *this is* and waiting to find out.

In today's key verse, the original verbiage *This is* denotes we are on the edge of our seats, expectant for what is to be revealed. The two words together refer to what will follow; they set the stage for the exciting and anticipated message. It is present tense and time inclusive. It is not *was*; it is not *will be*; it is always, now.

This *This is* message is for "Everyone who believes that Jesus is the Christ…" (1 John 5:1). If this is you, then listen up! The *This is* is about to be revealed. This message is for those who fear the Lord, who say they love God. He is a good Father—He does not leave His children in the dark. He commands us to love Him, but He also reveals how this *this is* is accomplished.

"This is love for God: to obey his commands…" (1 John 5:3). There it is—the mystery to what *This is* truly is! Loving God is not about doing things for Him, meeting the needs of others, or giving our time, talent, and treasures, although they are His commands to obey, when they stand alone, they do not fully prove or indicate we love God.

Loving God obeys God.

I often say one of the things I love about God's Word is He never leaves us in the dark. If He commands it, He directs it. If He expects it, He also exposes the know-how. Remember, God says what He means, and He means and does what He says. Therefore, nothing was left out of His Word, and nothing needs to be added. It is complete as it is. In 1 John 5:3, He reveals what *This is*, but then He takes it a step further. Because He wants to explain Himself? No, because out of His great love for His children, He will never sabotage our walk of faith. After it is revealed that obeying His commands is love for God, John says, "And his commands are not burdensome."

In your life if you have ever felt like His statutes are rigid or thought they were hard to carry out or you were led to believe they are impossible to manage, then your feelings and thoughts had you believe an untruth. The truth is, just because you think it or feel it does not make it true.

God's commands are not burdensome—they will never weigh heavy; they will not press down on you with oppressive force; they will not leave you unable to function. After all, His yoke is easy, and His burden is light (Matthew 11:30).

KEY CHALLENGE TO DAILY STAND: Check and see if the heaviness in your heart, mind, or soul is misguided feelings regarding God's commands.

Day 7

EVIL Spelled Backward

KEY VERSE: *Let those who love the Lord hate evil…Psalm 97:10*

A couple of years ago, I had coffee with a woman I met through social media. We had some pertinent things in common, so we decided to meet. It was a good idea. Hours separate us geographically, but on the things that matter, we were kindred spirits. However, gratefully I learned a huge lesson that day.

We were both using the same words to describe our Christian stance on some cultural issues but applying a couple of them quite differently. For instance, I used *conservative* in reference to how I was raised, and she assumed I meant no tattoos, no dancing, and no makeup. But that was off base from how I applied the word.

When we use perplexing words or phrases around newer Christians but do not explain them, we do them a disservice. Or, it could be you were raised in a strict church setting and have a skewed perspective on theological concepts. (Some people refer to the big words and phrases as Christian-ese.) We must be careful and intentional about how we say and explain such things.

Two Christian-ese words that get misconstrued and misinterpreted are holiness and righteousness. God calls His children to abide with and live out both standards.

Our early church experience or what we were brought up to believe and understand about God's standards depends on how we were raised. We tend to bristle or tuck in tight to Jesus.

Holiness allows every aspect of our life to be set apart and useful for God's purposes, it is an all-in, surrendered life to the Lord. It does not mean we need to quit our job and move to a third-world country to begin a mission, unless, of course, God calls us to that. Holiness gets lived out throughout our everyday life: at work, at home, in our community, in conversation, and through action.

Righteousness lives right: ethically, morally, and spiritually. God imputed and attributed righteousness to Abraham (Romans 4:18-22). The man stood firm in his faith: he believed the promises of God and he wholeheartedly trusted the Lord. He accepted God's will for his life and fully depended on God to lead and guide him along the way.

Psalm 97:10 summons us to hate evil. If we say we love the Lord, we must hate evil and choose to live in holiness and desire to have God impute righteousness our way. We tend to refer to the big sins as evil, but God calls all sin evil. And sin has a starting point: it begins with the devil, Mr. D-evil. He is evil, completely, and utterly evil. The earth is Satan's playground; we live in enemy territory. Jesus turns evil around. In Jesus, we find life. In Him we can have abundant life—to truly live as He intends (John 10:10). EVIL spelled backward is LIVE.

To be holy and righteous we must understand and accept that evil is all around us. To hate evil, we must know there is a right way to live.

If we utterly hate something we have zero desire to accept it, welcome it, invite it, feed it, negotiate with it, or embrace it.

When we completely love God, we have a deep desire to accept Him, welcome His Spirit, invite Jesus in, feast on His Word, obey His commands, and fully embrace all God has in store for us.

KEY POINT TO DAILY STAND: To love God we cannot accommodate sin.

Day 8

Displays Have the Say

KEY VERSE: *Love the Lord your God...Deuteronomy 6:5*

Before marriage I was involved as a leader in full-time youth ministry. One of the most helpful habits I instituted during that time was to view a teen's bedroom. With parental permission as I visited the student in their home, I peeked in their room. Getting a glimpse of the knick-knacks scattered about and what hung on the walls revealed their priorities and commitments—what music they liked, what superstars influenced them, and who or what had their attention and allegiance.

Today, I use the same motivation when I am invited to the home of other Christians. The décor speaks volumes about priority, influence, and loyalty. Likewise, it is vastly important to me that Kevin and my home reflects our lifestyle. If we say we love Jesus, people should be able to tell. If we declare we have a Biblical worldview, artwork and decorations should communicate that. If the Word of God is what we stand on and live by, some Scripture references should be present.

Godly living must include the things of God. There should be proof within our homes that we love God. That does not mean we need to have the New Testament inscribed on the wallpaper, or the Ten Commandments displayed in our front yard, or a life-sized depiction of the Last Supper attached to our roof. You and your family will benefit from placing godly reminders and spiritual declarations around your home.

Currently, I am at our little summer place. By little, I mean there is 800 square feet of pure relaxation and comfort surrounding me. From my small writing desk, as I glance to the right, two pieces of wall art are displayed. One has portions of 1 Corinthians chapter thirteen. The other boldly declares *TRUST IN THE LORD*. Most people drive golf carts around our summer community. As they come from a certain direction, suspended on the side of our golf cart garage hangs a piece of metal art declaring, *As for me and my house, we will serve the Lord.* We do not display or hang Christian themes to emphasize us; rather, Kevin and I desire to point others to Jesus and remind ourselves who we live for.

The challenge for you is—can others tell you love God by stepping into your home or onto your property?

Remember, in Deuteronomy Moses renews the covenant and reminds the people of God's love and His promises, His expectations, and His commands. They were told once again to love the Lord their God with all their hearts, souls, and strength (Deuteronomy 6:5).

But then in Deuteronomy 6:7-9, Moses used powerful verbs and verbiage to inspire and influence the people to do what was necessary to remind themselves and to potentially prove to others they loved God. The same applies to us today:

- Impress them on your children.
- Talk about them when you sit at home.
- Talk about them when you walk along the road.
- Talk about them when you lie down.
- Talk about them when you get up.
- Tie them as symbols on your hands.
- Bind them on your forehead.
- Write them on the doorframes of your house.
- Write them on your gates.

As they are displayed, they prove to others and remind us that we love God with all our heart, all our soul, and all our strength.

KEY QUESTION TO DAILY STAND: When others come into your domain, what displays tell them that you love God?

There is a name I love to hear,
I love to sing its worth;
it sounds like music in my ear,
the sweetest name on earth.

O how I love Jesus,
O how I love Jesus,
O how I love Jesus,
because he first loved me!

"Oh, How I Love Jesus"
By: Fredrick Whitefield

Day 9

Ask for Directions

KEY VERSE: *May the Lord direct your hearts into God's love and Christ's perseverance. 2 Thessalonians 3:5*

    I enjoy reading and following maps—the folded paper type. Of course, GPS makes it much safer and easier, especially when driving, but I still love tracking a journey and figuring out directions with a map. Though it is rare, I have zero qualms about stopping to ask for directions.
    According to today's key verse from 2 Thessalonians, God has directions for us. Notice where they lead: into God's love and Christ's perseverance. Now that ought to be a desired destination for all followers of Jesus!

1. **The Lord directs**. The original word for the verb *directs* means to go straight by the most direct and sufficient route; it avoids all unnecessary delays without any loss of undue time or achievement.

2. **Into God's love**. The Lord guides us straight to His love without any deviation. If we get off track, it is because we diverted, not Him. When we *feel* like God does not love or accept us, He did not remove His love. If we *think* a manmade scheme or self-made strategies will take us to His love, we are deceived to believe and presume the wrong directions.

3. **Into Christ's perseverance**. Steadfastness. Endurance. Patience and quiet waiting. In other words, God enables us as He directs us to endure and remain under the hardships and challenges

that He allows in our life along our faith journey.

I say if often: it is the small words that make a big difference. Notice the word *into* from today's key verse. It implies a motion that goes right to the object. In this case our hearts are set in motion by the Lord for God's love and Christ's perseverance to penetrate our life for a particular purpose and specific result. It indicates the destination was achieved.

Though the Greek word is *kardia*, it is necessary to know *your hearts* in today's key verse does not refer to the organ that pumps blood. It is your inner person, the center and seat of your spiritual life, your soul or mind. God directs all of you—the fountain and seat of your thoughts, passions, desires, appetites, affections, purposes, and endeavors—to His love and Christ's perseverance.

There should never be a day or a moment when we neglect to seek God's directions. He sends our souls on a straight trajectory to His love and the perseverance of Christ. We must be mindful to stop and ask for His guidance; otherwise, our souls will get delayed, detoured, or deviated from His intended destination.

KEY POINT TO DAILY STAND: God's directions always lead to safety and security for our souls, even if they take us on a straight path to hardship and trouble.

Day 10

Protective Services

KEY VERSE: *...Spread your protection over them, that those who love your name may rejoice in you. Psalm 5:11*

When he was a little boy, my son, Andrew, was extremely afraid of bad weather, especially thunderstorms. My husband, however, loves a good thunderstorm. He will sit on a sheltered porch and watch it roll in, pour rain, and move out. Me? I am like Andrew: I do not like them.

But I never let my small children know. It was my responsibility to protect them and help them overcome their fears. One time, when Andrew was eight, a tornado touched down two miles from our house. I went into immediate action.

At the time we had four children, 9, 8, 6, and 4. They were all playing together, and I called the eldest to come to me alone. I told her to get her brothers, have them *hide* from me in Andrew's closet, and stay there until I *found* them. It worked! A quick game of hide-from-momma kept Andrew from seeing the tornado-warning on the TV, and all three boys thought they had pulled one over on me, while I was protecting them from danger.

God is a good Father; He protects His children. The key verse says He spreads His protection over those who love His name. Too many Christians beg for His protection while dishonoring His ways. We cannot love Him while discrediting His statutes. Loving the name of the Lord, also loves His ways. It begs the challenge: if you want His protection, you better love His name!

God's protection is a shelter, a roof, a covering over us. The word can also mean to screen. This imagery of protection is profound:

- In football a screen pass is a short pass to a receiver who is protected by a screen of blockers. Fellow receivers or offensive linemen become his cover.
- We have screens on our windows to protect the inside of our homes from things we do not want inside.

Though we use screens, they are not completely impenetrable. Defensive players from the opposing team can break though the offensive screen. And just this week, while at our summer place, because spring has sprung, a film of green pollen was all over the surfaces in the rooms with opened windows.

Spiritually speaking, God will use whatever protection He deems necessary. There are times He spreads a roof or shelter over our souls. But He also calls for screen protection—allowing some things through to test and teach us, not to damage us. Yes, at times, He protects through teachable moments.

A footnote in my Bible says the name of the Lord is the manifestation of His character. His name and His traits cannot be separated from the other. According to the beginning of Psalm 5:11, if we take refuge in Him, we can be glad and always sing for joy. Those are not automatic responses for those who dwell under His shelter, but for those who love His name, they can choose gladness and joy, no matter what comes through the screen.

KEY QUESTION TO DAILY STAND: How will you pray for godly protection differently knowing it may be a testing ground of your faith?

Day 11

Security

KEY VERSE: *May those who love you be secure. Psalm 122:6*

We believe a lot of things bring security that is not trustworthy. Pension plans, bank accounts, and trust funds. People, plans, and professions. Ideologies, feelings, and manmade promises. All have the capacity for good, but we should not stake our security on any of them.

Let us take note on what the key verse does *not* say:

- May those who attend church be secure
- May those with deep pockets be secure
- May those who volunteer be secure
- May those who preach and teach be secure
- May those who are good be secure
- May those who are without sin be secure

Security is all about loving the Lord. That is where we find peace. The King Kames Version uses the word prosper in place of security. "…they shall prosper that love thee" (Psalm 122:6). The word means to be at ease, tranquil, or quiet. Those who love the Lord live in ease and with tranquility as security. The flip side is we live careless, thoughtless lives, and we will go astray.

In Psalm 122:6, before King David mentions security, he says, "Pray for the peace of Jerusalem…" He exhorts and encourages God's people to pray and gives them a suggestion for their supplication. Jerusalem was the royal city, plus it was known as the city of the Lord.

In America we have a democracy, not a dynasty; however, it is our duty as a citizen of heaven to pray for our nation's peace and prosperity—not to be the greatest nation on earth, but to have significant and godly influence in the world. Our money still declares *in God we trust*; therefore, as Christians who indeed trust the Lord, we should also love the Lord and follow the Psalmist's advice to pray for our government and leadership.

We spend an exorbitant amount of time pleading to God for peace. And by that we mean, the absence of trouble and removal of threats. We pray for what God already supplied through Jesus. God's Word expresses why we need Jesus:

- Jesus Himself was clear when He said we would have trouble (John 16:33).
- Paul spoke outright when he said if we want to live a godly life in Jesus, we will be persecuted (2 Timothy 3:12).
- And Peter stated we are blessed as we suffer for what is right (1 Peter 3:14).

Yes! Indeed, we need Jesus!

Lasting peace comes only through Jesus, the Prince of Peace. As we love Jesus and remain in Him, we will know true security by His presence, which brings us peace. It can be found no other way.

KEY THOUGHT TO DAILY STAND: If you look for peace in anything other than Jesus, it is false security.

Day 12

God is Love

KEY VERSE: *And so we know and rely on the love God has for us...1 John 4:16a*

We cannot know the love of God apart from Jesus. And we cannot love God without Jesus. He is the bridge that crosses the chasm between God and humanity.

The bookends to our key verse say, "If anyone acknowledges that Jesus is the Son of God, God lives in him and he in God" and "God is love. Whoever lives in love lives in God, and God in him" (1 John 4:15 and 1 John 4:16b). For God to make His dwelling in us, we must acknowledge Jesus. Simultaneously, for us to live in God we must live in love.

The Bible is His Word; therefore, the words are ordered exactly as God intended. In today's current Christian culture, there are some who confuse God and love. In this Scripture three words are very clear: God is love.

But some swap two of the words making it *Love is God*. We do not have license to change God's Word. But through accountability comes liability. God's Word is the authority for our life. It says God is love. Therefore, that is our filter and foundation.

1 John 5:16 begins with the most common conjunction found in the New Testament.

If.

Over nine thousand times God purposefully uses this conjunction to make connections. We can know and rely on the love God has for us, but first only *if* we acknowledge—confess, declare, admit, and agree that Jesus is the Son.

Knowing the love of God does not come from what we have heard about Him, it is through personal experience and first-hand acquaintance. Paul said, "I want to know

Christ and the power of his resurrection..." (Philippians 3:10). The *know* in this verse is the same word in today's key verse. First-hand acquaintance with Jesus requires dying to self to live as He intends.

Relying on the love of God is being confident in and persuaded by the Lord. We do not rely on His love by mustering the desire or ability; we rely on His love by acknowledging, confessing, declaring, admitting, and agreeing that Jesus is the Son of God. Thereby, God lives in us, and we live in Him.

And in the same manner, when we live in love we live in God, and He lives in us. After all, God is love. We can know this and rely on it!

KEY POINT TO DAILY STAND: We are either persuaded by Christ or swayed by culture.

Day 13

Spiritual Surgery

KEY VERSE: *The Lord your God will circumcise your hearts…so that...Deuteronomy 30:6*

    I have many examples I could note from when I was an immature youngster who caused a ruckus in Sunday School class or youth group. Suffice it to say, at times, I contributed comments that prompted my friends to giggle and squirm through embarrassing and awkward topics.

    Frankly, even as adults, there are just some matters we are uncomfortable talking about. But if it is in God's Word, they cannot be overlooked, avoided, or neglected. Circumcision is one of those topics. But before we view it as a physical or medical modification that makes us squirm and giggle like a middle schooler, we must discard our unease and apply spiritual vision to circumcision.

    Let us divide Deuteronomy 30:6 into three parts:

- "The Lord your God will circumcise your hearts…"
- "…so that you may love him…"
- "…with all your heart and with all your soul, and live."

    First, notice the middle segment. When a *so that* appears in Scripture, purpose follows. The purpose in this verse is to love the Lord. Now, look at the first part of the verse and notice the directive: circumcise your hearts. And finally, take note of how to triumph (all-in love) in the purpose, plus the result (we may live) of the purpose.

    The verse ends with a promise. *You may live* means a high degree of bliss combined with spiritual blessing. Question: Who would circumvent that?! Answer: Those who ignore and avoid the first part of the verse. Circumcision of the heart averts circumvention on our faith journey.

There are behaviors that keep us from faithfully walking by faith. Doubt, worry, fear, hesitation, insecurity, unwillingness, unforgiveness, bitterness, rebellion, wildness, folly—the list goes on. These indiscretions and transgressions stand between our soul and wholeheartedly loving our Lord.

Our souls need spiritual surgery!

To perform circumcision on our heart, there is no need to call for an appointment or to spend time in the waiting room. The Great Physician already predetermined the appointment, and He is always in and eternally prepared to operate and cut off what is in the way of keeping us from living as Jesus intends.

If we focus more on *you may live* but avoid the part that says *all your heart* and *all your soul*, then we cannot live out the purpose of circumcision: to love the Lord fully and completely. Too many Christians want to live as a follower of Jesus without responding to the command to call on the Great Physician. Only when we allow the Lord access to perform the spiritual surgery required for our souls, will we wholeheartedly love God.

KEY CHALLENGE TO DAILY STAND: We expect a great deal from the Great Physician, so consider what areas of your life need to be cut off so you can fully and completely love Him.

Day 14

Just Because

KEY VERSE: *I love the Lord…Psalm 116:1*

Being around children is always an eye-opening experience. If we are paying attention, their words and actions will cause us to laugh, smile, point out childlike perspectives, and often lead to teaching moments.

Between the ages of two through five, *why* is a common question. Imagine if we responded, "Just because," to their innocent questions:

- Why can't I touch the stove?
- Why does my baby brother cry?
- Why do I have to go to bed?
- Why is it raining?
- Why do you hug me so much?

Children need explanations to fulfill their curiosity and help them understand the world around them. When my children were young, I loved answering their questions. They needed straight and honest answers. *Just because* hardly ever suffices, especially to one of my favorite questions. "Mommy, why do you love me?"

In Psalm 116:1-6, the Psalmist begins verse one, "I love the Lord," and ends verse six with, "…he saved me." However, we do not find *just because* sandwiched between. Before you read why the Psalmist loves the Lord, how would you answer the question:

Why do you love the Lord?

It is a good lesson for us to respond to this question with more than *just because*. The Psalmist gave detail on why he loves God. Because:

- He heard his voice (Psalm 116:1).
- He heard his cry for mercy (116:1).
- He turned His ear to him (Psalm 116:2).
- He is available (Psalm 116:4).
- He is gracious (Psalm 116:5).
- He is righteous (Psalm 116:5).
- He is full of compassion (Psalm 116:5).
- He protects (Psalm 116:6).
- He saves (Psalm 116:6).

At times, though it is acceptable to recognize what God has done for us, we need a check in our spirit to make sure our personal provision is not the only reason we love Him. Focusing on what qualities of God carry us through hard times or have our attention through hardship go beyond *just because*.

If we began every day with an *I love the Lord because He saved me* mindset, it would profoundly influence our choices. And if we daily pondered why we love the Lord, it would unquestionably inspire our walk of faith and cause our love for God to grow deeper.

KEY QUESTION TO DAILY STAND: Why do you love God?

Day 15

Undeniable Love

KEY VERSE: *Jesus said, '…do you truly love me more than…do you truly love me…do you love me…' John 21:15-17*

    A man and wife once shared about the time they confronted one set of their parents. Over the first few years of marriage, they were confused about why the parents would say, "You know I love you," instead of letting "I love you," stand-alone as three powerful words that declaratively communicated their love to their adult children. The man inquired, "Why do you insert *you know* before you say I love you?"

    You know altered the claim. Oh, the man and his wife knew they were loved, but to them, hearing *you know* changed the declaration from an affirming assertion to a questionable intent. The challenge changed the parents. From that day forward, they simply said, "I love you," and the man and his wife were assured and confident they were loved.

    In John 21:15-17, three times Jesus said to Peter, "Do you love me?" Grammatically we may prefer *asks* instead of *said* since Jesus did ask Peter a question. But in the original language, the word that is used for said, means *to say*.

    But that is not the main point.

    Three times Jesus confronted Peter:

- Do you truly love me more than…?
- Do you truly love me?
- Do you love me?

And three times Peter responded:

- Yes, Lord, you know that I love you.
- Yes, Lord, you know that I love you.
- Lord, you know all things; you know that I love you.

Days earlier, Peter had massively failed. Three times he denied the Christ and three times a rooster crowed to announce each occurrence (John 18:15-18; 25-27). Prior to disowning Jesus, Peter followed Him at a distance (Matthew 26:58; Mark 14:54).

Distant disciples are positioned to disown their Lord.

After the resurrection Peter went from denying Christ to being a fully devoted follower, and from following at a distance, to being tucked in tight to Jesus. And then Jesus affirmed Peter's devotion and confirmed his call by entrusting him to, "Feed my sheep" (John 21:17c).

Before disciples of Jesus can love His people, they must first love Him. Three times Jesus inquired about Peter's love. There is no coincidence of three denials and three inquiries. Jesus was not rubbing Peter's face in his recent act of repudiation. No! Rather, the disciple was given the opportunity to grieve over his past sin—not to feel bad and sit in guilt, but to see pardoned sin and to be reminded of the amazing grace of a beautiful Savior and Lord.

Peter's third emphatic claim, "Lord, you know all things; you know that I love you," (John 21:17b) points to a forgiving, gracious, merciful, sovereign, redemptive, restorative, and eternally loving Savior!

KEY QUESTION TO DAILY STAND: Jesus asks you, "Do you truly love me?" What is your honest response?

Day 16

Exceptions are Not Exemptions

KEY VERSE: *Solomon showed his love for the Lord by walking according to the statutes of his father David, except that…1 Kings 3:3*

    The other day I was driving our golf cart around the grounds of our summer place. The cart in front of me was going a bit slow, but since the park rules say the speed limit is ten miles per hour, they were not going excessively slow. However, the man driving the cart behind me got impatient as he apparently thought he was an exception to the rule. He executed his plan and passed me, but just as he was about to pass the cart in front of me, the statement *policy protects* rang true.

    At the same time he was about to pass the other cart, the lady put out her left hand to indicate she was making a left turn. It was a good thing Mr. Exception-to-the-rule was paying attention, otherwise, I would have witnessed an accident.

    Now I am not a Public Safety Officer, but as the man was right next to me, I did exclaim, "And that's why we have rules to follow." Though he drove on as if nothing was amiss, his self-appointed exception did not make him exempt from following the rules.

    Exceptions cause more harm than good. Spiritually, they keep our journey inconsistent; we become unsteady, and we waver on our walk of faith.

    It is noted in 1 Kings 3:3 that King Solomon showed his love for the Lord. But in the same verse, it states there was an exception to his devotion. This is inconsistent. Covenant love must not share soul space, and it cannot have exceptions to the rules. Solomon offered sacrifices and burned incense on the high places—sacrilegious places of worship. The high places were where pagan worship took place. Solomon walked away from the statutes that referenced acceptable worship and *that directed* where and how to build altars to the Lord he claimed to love.

God initiated a covenant relationship with His people. We can read specifically through the book of Judges, 1st and 2nd Chronicles, and 1st and 2nd Kings about how God's people wavered and blatantly sinned when they made exceptions to His rules. God's commands protect. They are not boundaries to keep us bound up and held back from living well. They are not limitations to limit us from good things.

My husband has never told me, "Babe, I love you, except…" or "I'm devoted to you, except…" Of course, since 1988, I know there are things about me that have annoyed or bothered him, but he has never used them as exceptions to withhold his vows of covenant.

Again, loving God means doing His will, His way. There are no exceptions to His rules. When it comes to following His commands, He makes no exemptions for any of His children. Same Father, same expectations for all.

KEY POINT TO DAILY STAND: Loving God, loves all His statutes, with no exceptions.

Day 17

Tabernacle Time

KEY VERSE: *I love the house where you live, O Lord, the place where your glory dwells. Psalm 26:8*

On Day 4 of Love God, I mentioned how I responded to the invitation to invite Jesus into my heart at a wooden altar. Though it no longer exists, I love the memory of that old tabernacle!

In 1997 my family first attended Family Camp. Situated and centrally located on the grounds sits the wooden tabernacle that was once the grandstand of an old horse track. Over the years Kevin and I have been challenged and changed when the Holy Spirit ushered us to the altar many times in that place. We love that tabernacle!

For a few years Kevin and I had the privilege of being the overseers and leaders of Family Camp. Each evening throughout the weekly camp, everyone present gathers in the tabernacle. One night, as Kevin was opening the worship service, he introduced a catchy question that continues to be asked. "Hey, Bay Shore Camp, what time is it?" And the people loudly respond, "It's Tabernacle Time!"

Before Kevin asked the question that first night, he taught that the word tabernacle is not only a noun but also a verb. He stressed how Jesus desires to tabernacle within us. He challenged the worshipers to consider what else might be within the place where the glory of the Lord is meant to dwell.

Years ago Robert Boyd Munger wrote a mini-book that burst into the Christian market and is still available today. *My Heart—Christ's Home* has the reader imagine their heart as the house where Jesus lives and to consider if He is allowed access to the different spaces.

In Psalm 26:8 the writer states he loves the house

where God lives. When we welcome Jesus into our lives, He desires full access. As Jesus sits on the throne of our souls, then it is a place where He tabernacles and where His glory dwells. And we should love that!

In the original language *the place* where His glory *dwells* means dwelling place or tabernacle. In the Old Testament the people were assured of His presence in the tabernacle, the temple of the Lord. His glory indicated His very presence. The House of the Lord is His residence, a place where He settles.

I knew a person who refused to invite the Lord into a certain place in her life. She said, "He can have access to all of me, just not this space." Consequently, she exchanged His dwelling for her sinful desire. Sadly, He cannot tabernacle there.

KEY QUESTIONS TO DAILY STAND: Can Jesus tabernacle in your heart? Is your soul a tabernacle where you love the Lord? How does the glory of the Lord dwell in your life?

Day 18

Stress Test

KEY VERSE: *If anyone says, 'I love God,' but hates his brother, he is a liar…1 John 4:20*

Have you ever noticed that spectators at a baseball game cheer in repetition? *Hey batter, batter! Swing batter, swing! Over the plate pitcher, over the plate!* It is acceptable, even appreciated, when the fans repeat themselves.

If I had a dollar for every time I repeated myself as a parent—well, let us just leave it at that. And yet, at times, repetition can be a necessary and beneficial strategy.

John, one of the first disciples of Jesus, repetitively mentions love in his letter 1 John to the believers in Jesus. John had an appreciation for repetition. In 1 John 4:7-21 the word love is written almost thirty times!

But he also had a theme to stress.

In the passage there is a sort of *Stress Test for Believers*—to evaluate if we grasp the significance of intention when we proclaim we love God. First, John stresses the love of God and our love towards one another. He says God showed us love, and he emphasizes God loved us first, and he reminds us we ought to love one another (1 John 4:9-11).

And then in 1 John 4:20, we find the stress test: *anyone who does not love his brother…cannot love God.* Before you answer a pertinent question, let us first be clear, when John refers to *brothers*, he means fellow believers. All Christians are a part of the family of God. We are brothers and sisters together.

Next, about hatred. Though it is inconceivable, at times, Christians hurt one another. Unfortunately, the church is not absent of victims, nor perpetrators. There is not one space on earth that can hold everyone who has been hurt by a fellow believer. We are a massive multitude. Though we cannot control another's behavior, we are liable for any hatred we harbor in our hearts.

Holding someone accountable for the despicable actions toward you is acceptable and appropriate; hatred is not. Manipulation and mistreatment; distress and damage; insult and injury; cruelty and corruption are horrible and hurtful, but hatred is never justifiable.

No matter the level of hurt, we are all evaluated and held accountable under John's *Stress Test for Believers*. God gives us this command. "Whoever loves God must also love his brother" (1 John 4:21). Our love for God enables us to love everyone. John stressed that when we love others, we love God. Loving them does not mean we need to be in fellowship with them, or in the same zip code as them, or share a pew with them. Loving them is an act of obedience to the One we love.

Do you harbor hatred in your heart? If you do then it is your relationship with God that gets harmed. Release the hurt to the Lord; allow Him to soften your heart so you can live as Jesus intends—in obedience to the Lord.

KEY POINT TO DAILY STAND: Do not be stressed by hurt; rather, be obedient to the Lord.

Day 19

Sonrise

KEY VERSE: *...may they who love you be like the sun...Judges 5:31*

In 1969 the Beatles released their hit song "Here Comes the Sun." Today it is one of the most streamed songs from the enormously popular band. George Harrison wrote the catchy tune inspired by the long England winters that felt like they would never end.

And perhaps we are all familiar with Annie's song that tells us what to do when we are "stuck with a day that's gray and lonely." The red-headed, determined girl maintains to "just stick out my chin and grin." After all, the sun will come up tomorrow. Of course, we all know the sun can shine on winter days. And though heavy cloud cover hides the sun, it still shines bright above the clouds.

Years ago on Easter morning, it was more common than now to have a *Sonrise Service*. I remember as a child, just as the sun rose, we gathered on the sidewalk outside our church, and I watched my mom stand on the roof with other trumpeters and brass musicians as they played and presented a fanfare rejoicing Jesus had risen!

Cloudy or not, the sunrise is not an indicator that God's Son did rise.

Judges 5:2-31 is a poetic song to commemorate and celebrate the victory God's people had over Sisera, the commander of Jabin's army, a king in Canaan. The land was a part of the Promise that years earlier God declared belonged to His people. He commanded Deborah, who led the people at that time, that it was time to take the land. (The detailed account is found in Judges chapter four.)

As Deborah concluded her praise to the Lord through song, she prayed that the people who love God would be like the sun. The message is clear:

- No matter the season, the sun still shines.
- No matter the storm on earth, the sun still shines.
- No matter what the day holds, the sun still rises.
- When the sun sets, it still shines elsewhere.
- The sun sheds light.
- The sun shines bright.
- The sun feeds and nourishes.
- The sun promotes growth.

Deborah prayed a good prayer! May those of us who love God be like the sun!

There is another song that perhaps is not familiar to you, but the little chorus I learned as a child still rings true today.

A sunbeam, a sunbeam,
Jesus wants me for a sunbeam
A sunbeam, a sunbeam,
I'll be a sunbeam for Him.

If we love God, we will be a ray of sunlight to those who walk in darkness. Likewise, we should follow the words of Jesus when He taught His disciples, "Let your light shine…" (Matthew 5:16).

KEY CHALLENGE TO DAILY STAND: We have a choice: be like the sun or live under the clouds.

Day 20

Past Problems

KEY VERSE: *The Lord appeared to us in the past, saying: I have loved you…I have drawn you…Jeremiah 31:3*

There are times we need to back the train up. This is one of my favorite concepts and a recurring theme as I speak to people dealing with issues that have them stuck on their faith journey. When we attempt to deal with what *appears* to be wrong but find zero solutions or freedom, that is when it is time to back the train up to look and see if something previous got us off the rails.

Some folks are afraid or anxious because they think backing up the train goes back, but looking back is not going back. Looking back notices and grabs facts. And when we have the facts, we have the truth. When we have the truth, we can properly and wisely deal with the derailment—if we go to God for His counsel and allow His Word to speak to our situation.

Jeremiah was a prophet sent from God to speak His truth to God's people. He corrected them, rebuked them, and reminded them about where they derailed and what they needed to do to get back on track.

In Jeremiah 31 the prophet spoke of restoration. God's people were in captivity because they fell off the spiritual track God had intended and provided for them, but God always remembers the covenant He made with His people. And there was always a remnant of followers who remained faithful. Jeremiah 31:2 refers to them as, "The people who survive the sword…" Even if they were held captive some remained righteous.

Jeremiah goes on and speaks God's words. "…I will come to give rest…" For anyone stuck on their faith journey or caught in bondage to past pain or past sin, they need and crave God's rest. This rest is prearranged and provided by God; He grants it and He gives it.

At times we derail because we determine and divvy out our idea of rest. That is not our concern. True rest is God's idea; therefore, He plans and assigns it. Jeremiah gave the promise of rest, but before they were set free, the people needed to look back.

God reminded them of His love. The King James Version says, "Yea, I have loved thee with an everlasting love: therefore with lovingkindness have I drawn thee" (Jeremiah 31:3).

God's love is everlasting—not from this day forward; rather, He always has; He currently is, and He will always love His people. And it is His lovingkindness and goodness that drew them back to Him.

His love pursues us. His love holds us. His love draws us back when we get off track. God always initiates! God always pursues! God always loves! God always draws His faithful followers back into the fold.

We need to look back and be reminded that He never stopped loving us! He did not push us off track! And any derailment is on us, but it is His lovingkindness that draws us back.

KEY POINT TO DAILY STAND: God loves you right where you are, but He loves you too much to leave you there.

Day 21

Proving Ground

KEY VERSE: *...The Lord your God is testing you to find our whether you love him with all your heart and with all your soul. Deuteronomy 13:3*

The first time I left a child home alone, my eldest was eleven years old. I went to the corner store with the younger three children to buy a gallon of milk. She was home alone a total of eight minutes. That first test proved she could be trusted with my short absence. However, that age and timeframe did not set a precedence for my other five children. Additional tests proved each one would qualify for their turn at being home alone based on other variables.

A good teacher tests their students. To see who fails? No. Test results prove the student caught what the teacher taught.

In Romeo, Michigan, on nearly four thousand acres of land sits one site of the Ford Proving Grounds. It is used for the development and validation testing of new vehicles. A high-speed track and over one hundred miles of special roads with varying surfaces and grades are just a part of the testing ground for each vehicle that is put to the test.

God has proving grounds for His people, and He sanctions tests for them. They prove if we are faithful, and they also check for faulty and unfaithful following. Spiritual tests show if we love Him, serve Him, observe His commands, and walk in all His ways.

However, there are times we misread a test as an act of Satan, blaming him for hard times. But what if the hardship is a test of our holiness? Sometimes we incorrectly refer to God's proving ground as Satan's playground. Oh, yes! Satan does mess with us; that is a certainty! It is called temptation. But God's Word is clear; though He tests us, He will never tempt us (James 1:13).

In Deuteronomy 13, Moses is talking to God's chosen people. This chapter does not begin with a new thought, so let us see it as if Moses took a breath and kept talking. He warns the people that if someone comes along and tries to convince them to follow other gods, they were not to listen to those words or heed the advice. And then he said, "…The Lord your God is testing you…"

The test would prove or disprove if they:

- Loved God with all their heart (Deuteronomy 13:3).
- Loved God with all their soul (Deuteronomy 13:3).
- Followed God (Deuteronomy 13:4).
- Revered God (Deuteronomy 13:4).
- Kept God's commands (Deuteronomy 13:4).
- Obeyed God (Deuteronomy 13:4).
- Served God (Deuteronomy 13:4).
- Held fast to God (Deuteronomy 13:4).

Our love for God must be put to the test. It will prove where we are faithful or where we have failed. Either way, a test from God proves His great love for us. If we are tucked in tight to Jesus, we are safe and secure. And if we are not, His test will show us we need to get back to where we belong.

KEY THOUGHT TO DAILY STAND: Pressure tests from God reveal leaky faith and prove we need Jesus, the Solid Rock; after all, all other ground is sinking sand.

Day 22

To Wait is Not a Heavy Weight

KEY VERSE: *Keep yourselves in God's love as you wait for…Jude 21*

Waiting is something every human does, but it is also something we struggle to do well. Losing weight is hard work with positive benefits. Likewise, waiting on the Lord may be hard work, but the spiritual gains are eternal.

A lot of Christians are familiar with how God says to wait:

- Be still and wait (Psalm 37:7).
- I waited patiently for the Lord (Psalm 40:1).
- Wait on the Lord; be strong and take heart (Psalm 27:14).

God expects we will wait, and He tells us how. The problem comes when we consider waiting a heavy burden. But God's waits do not weigh heavy. When we are in His waiting room, it is not because He is not ready to do a good work in us; rather, it is because we need some holy prescription or soul surgery.

Jude is a short book of the Bible, containing twenty-five verses, yet it has powerful and impactful messages. In the first verse we read who the recipients of the letter are, "…to those…who are loved by God…and kept by Jesus Christ."

Loved by God; kept by Jesus. Notice today's key verse. Jude uses *love* and *keep* again. He persuades us to keep in God's love. The word kept (Jude 1) and *keep* (Jude 21) are the same Greek word. It means to preserve and spiritually guard.

How do we wait before we graduate to glory? How

do we live before the Lord Jesus Christ calls us to our eternal home? We remain in God's love where our relationship with Jesus is maintained, preserved, and guarded. It is up to us to watch over our spiritual growth and keep it intact.

Let us not overlook that we can only keep ourselves in God's love because He first loved us and provided the way into His love—through Jesus Christ.

Jude 24 uses the word keep again, only this time it is a different Greek word. Jude says, "To him who is able to *keep* you from falling…" Yes, it is our duty to keep ourselves in God's love, but it is the oversight and reliability and trustworthiness of Jesus to keep us from falling. This *keep* is an uninterrupted and unbroken vigilance with a deeply personal interest to keep watch over and to keep secure. We are incapable of keeping this kind of guard over ourselves.

It is not our love for God that we remain in; it is His love for us we are called to keep ourselves in so that we have the vigilant and personal protection of Jesus that keeps us from falling as we wait for our call to go home.

KEY QUESTION TO DAILY STAND: Have your waits been heavy? If so, what heaviness needs to be laid at the feet of Jesus?

Day 23

Life Preserver

KEY VERSE: *Love the Lord, all his saints! The Lord preserves the faithful…Psalm 31:23*

When one of my sons was little, he was afraid to swim. We often went to our friend's pond, and Troy always wanted to wear a life jacket. His favorite was the red one. He would put his skinny arms in the holes and come to me to buckle it up tight. One time, while wading in shallow waters, the clasp that goes between his legs came undone, and he panicked as the vest began to rise over his head.

Good thing Daddy was close by. In one strong swoop he grabbed our boy, pulled him close, reattached the buckle, and made sure he felt safe before he released him to play in the water once again.

There are many forms of floatation devices, but most are not adequate for lifesaving. For instance, take inflatable armbands, also called water wings. Though they help keep children afloat in a pool, they would not be the right choice as a lifeline for the one swept overboard in the deep waters of an open sea.

Though life jackets and water wings are referred to as life preservers, only God preserves life. And yet, not all lives. According to Psalm 31:23, He preserves the faithful. Who are the faithful? The Psalmist answers they are saints of the Lord. Who are the saints of the Lord? The first phrase of today's key verse says those who love the Lord!

The following bullet points are the original meanings of four words from Psalm 31:23:

- Love: beloved; the same great love God has for His children
- Saints: godly, good, holy, kind, pious

[denotes they belong to God]
- Preserves: to watch, guard, keep, preserve, protect
- Faithful: confirmed trusted and certain, assured safe and secure, a continual steadfastness

Using these definitions, I paraphrase the key verse this way:

All you who belong to the Lord,
who clearly show your deep love for Him
through word and deed.
You who live godly, kind, and pious lives,
revenant, devoted, and earnest in all God's ways.
Because you are steadfast and God has confirmed
the certainty of your faith,
be assured
His watchful eye is on you,
His everlasting arm guards you,
and He preserves, protects, and keeps you.

KEY CHALLENGE TO DAILY STAND: Hey, saints—faithfully love the Lord! He is our life preserver.

Day 24

Pleading Prayers

KEY VERSE: *...Oh, Lord the great and awesome God, who keeps his covenant of love with all who love him and obey his commands...Daniel 9:4*

A few years ago Kevin and I attended a prayer retreat. As an extrovert I was somewhat apprehensive because I assumed we would not have much opportunity to socialize with the other participants. However, any reluctance on my part did not last long. The weekend was filled with many opportunities to connect with people and engage in lengthy discussions. I was encouraged and challenged by solid Biblical teaching, and I met Paula, who became my prayer partner.

For a couple of years, Paula and I connected every few weeks to share prayer concerns and to pray with one another. Though our prayer connection lasted for a season, it still has a great impact on my life. Paula influenced my prayer life in special ways and modeled to me how to plead to the Lord.

Too often, followers of Jesus pray like we are in line at a fast-food restaurant. We place an order with the Lord, pull up to His holy window, and expect Him to hand over the requested item.

But we are to follow the two-word directive from Paul (1 Thessalonians 5:17). Pray continually. That means incessantly and without ceasing. Intercession has no intermission, so keep on praying!

Prayer has many methods and models, but pleading prayers are the focus for today. I am not sure who to credit, but some time ago I learned two types of what I call *pleading prayers*:

- Travailing Prayer: unceasingly praying until new life is birthed into a circumstance
- Prevailing Prayer: deep petitions and hovering and covering supplications

Supplication is an appeal, a request, a plea. Paula pleaded on my behalf for a particular request. Someone close to me had walked away from their faith—do not mistake that they abandoned their faith; no—they just stopped walking with Jesus. And it had consequences. Lifestyle choices, recreational activities, attitude, motivation, and integrity were all negatively affected.

But, oh, for those travailing and prevailing prayers! Like Daniel, Paula and I turned to the Lord God and pleaded with him in prayer and petition (Daniel 9:3). We prayed like Daniel.

Lord, our great and awesome God, who keeps his covenant of love…even if we falter and fail, but praise Your great name, You do not! We confess on behalf of _____, for their sinful ways, their rebellion to You and Your ways. Thank You for being slow to anger, quickly come to this one. We plead to You, Lord, to bring conviction and awareness. Bother this one, hound this one, transform this one. In Jesus' Name, amen! (see Daniel 9:4-19).

Pleading and prevailing prayer works! This one we prayed for is now tucked back in tight to Jesus, loving God with their whole heart, serving Him faithfully, observing His commands, and walking in all His ways.

KEY THOUGHT TO DAILY STAND: What supplications do you have that could use prevailing and travailing prayer? Hover and cover them with pleading prayers to the great and awesome God who keeps His covenant of love with all who love Him and obey His commands.

Day 25

Agape

KEY VERSE: *Whoever has my commands and obeys them, he is the one who loves me. He who loves me will be loved by my Father, and I too will love him and show myself to him. John 14:21*

When reading the Bible I pay close attention to verbs and conjunctions. In today's key verse let us take note of four verbs and highlight one conjunction.

The Verbs:

- **Has**: to hold fast to and possess in the mind
- **Obeys**: properly maintain and keep; hold fast
- **Love**: it is choosing to love how God loves, through His power and direction. It is Christ living in and through us. It is being Jesus-with-skin-on.
- **Show**: to manifest, exhibit. It is to know through the Holy Spirit's intervention that Jesus is alive and in heaven, but at work in the souls of His disciples.

The Conjunction:

- **And**: even, also, namely (it never means however)
- **And I**: I also, I too

We are not responsible to come up with the commands that we are to obey. Throughout the Bible God clearly designates His commands and provides the *how-to* of how we follow them.

Obedience is a choice. But according to the definitions of the words previously stated, we cannot disconnect *having* them from *obeying* them. Similarly, when Jesus says He too will love, He also says He will exhibit that love in the one who loves Him back.

We serve a God of order, never chaos or confusion. Perhaps if you get confused by His ways, a better look at His order is called for. Take the key verse. Christians today are confused by love. We are consumed with who and what dictates and determines what love is and how we receive it.

Remember there are many different words to describe love in the Greek language. This verse uses only one. Agape love.

- Agape love sent Jesus to earth.
- Agape love demonstrates God's love for us.
- Agape love bridges the gap between sin and humanity.
- Agape love washed His disciples' feet.
- Agape love healed, freed the demoniacs, and loved the unlovable.
- Agape love sent His Son to the cross.
- Agape love hung on the cross.
- Agape love said, "Forgive them, they do not know what they are doing."
- Agape love showed His scars.
- Agape love loves His disciples.

True followers of Jesus show God they love Him by holding fast to His commands, possessing the mind of Christ (1 Corinthians 2:16b), and being Jesus-with-skin-on to the world around them.

Being in Christ comes only from Him being in us. And when we are in Christ, we are to do whatever He tells us (John 2:5). That is loving God and being loved by Jesus in return (John 14:15).

KEY POINT TO DAILY STAND: To obey is better than sacrifice (1 Samuel 15:22).

I love to tell the story
of unseen things above,
of Jesus and his glory,
of Jesus and his love.
I love to tell the story
because I know it's true;
it satisfies my longings
as nothing else can do.

"I Love to Tell the Story"
Kate Hankey

Day 26

Live Right

KEY VERSION: *For the Lord loves the just…Psalm 37:28*

A popular radio personality often says, "Now, go do the right thing." This tagline intrigues me. People call into her show looking for advice on many different matters. The consistent counsel or correction is always straightforward, blunt, and brusque. Though the mantra remains intact, to live right, encouragement is not enough.

Within each of us should be a holy conviction to do the right thing. However, news stories, real crime podcasts, full court dockets, and crowded jails and prisons prove that just because we are persuaded to do the right thing, it does not mean humanity complies.

Likewise, there are people all around us doing harm and not living right. They are in our neighborhoods, homes, workplaces, and yes, even in churches. If every pastor concluded their sermon by urging congregations to do the right thing without teaching and preaching God's way to righteousness, the people would leave with a recommendation, but not revelation.

Remember, God's Word reveals God's ways; therefore, to do good and live right we must go to His Word and live it out His way.

The key verse says God loves the just. Another way to say it is He loves what is right. The previous verse says, "Turn from evil and do good…" (Psalm 37:27). Sounds simple, right? Intentionality is never easy, but it is always necessary in doing right. And the Psalmist says God loves the one who does.

Yet, Psalm 37:28 continues, "…and [he] will not forsake his faithful ones." The word forsake means to leave or loosen. Faithful folks do good and live right. And God's promise to the faithful is He will remain close by and never loosen His grip on them.

But wait, there is more! Psalm 37:28 adds, "…They will be protected forever." Do not miss this eternal declaration! The faithful—those who do good and live right—will always have divine protection. They will be kept, guarded, and preserved by God.

When we truly love God, we will be compelled to do good. And when we do good, we live right. God loves the one who lives right. And He shows it by never forsaking and always protecting the ones He loves.

KEY POINT TO DAILY STAND: Loving God lives right.

Day 27

Careful Now!

KEY VERSE: *So be very careful to love the Lord your God. Joshua 23:11*

Across the front of the large deck at our summer place are three steps. Recently, my granddaughter, Moriah, was walking down the middle when she almost tripped, so I immediately pulled her close. Her big eyes looked up at mine and she smiled as I said, "Careful now, Sweetie." She obviously felt comforted by my closeness and calmed by my gentle caution.

Closeness and caution are just two valuable aspects and assurances of love. Because God's covenant love is the key source to life and is essential to our walk of faith, without it we would trip and fall, and falter and fail. It is a good thing God's Word is chock full of *careful now's*.

Our response to God's gentle cautions ought to be like Moriah's. Because God knows we are prone to wander on our faith journey, He talks about stumbling blocks and footholds, and He draws close to warn us to be careful:

- Be careful to do everything I have said (Exodus 23:13).
- We must pay more careful attention…so we do not drift away (Hebrews 2:1).
- So if you think you are standing firm, be careful that you don't fall (1 Corinthians 10:12).
- Give careful thought to your ways (Haggai 1:5).
- Be careful which foundation you build your life on (1 Corinthians 3:10-15).

Problems arise when we deduce the *careful now's* as disadvantages in our life. It has already been said, but it is worth repeating: our God is a good Father. He loves His children, but love cannot be absent of warning and caution.

Before he died, Joshua gave the leaders of Israel a farewell speech. He reminded them all that God did for their sake and how He fought on their behalf. He encouraged them that God would keep His promise about the Promised Land. In Joshua 23:6-11 we find some cautions the old man had for the people:

- Be very strong.
- Be very careful to obey all that was written in the Book of the Law without turning aside to the right or to the left.
- Be very careful to not associate with those who serve other gods; to not invoke their names, serve, or bow to those other gods.
- Be very careful to hold fast to the Lord because the Lord would fight for them.
- Be very careful to love the Lord who was their God.

And then Joshua concluded the speech by warning the people about what would happen if they violated the covenant of the Lord. He said God's anger would burn against them, and they would quickly perish from the good land (Joshua 23:16).

Following the book of Joshua is Judges, where we find cycles of disobedience and patterns of broken vows from the people of God. Twice in that book, it tells us what tripped them up, "In those days…everyone did as he saw fit" (Judges 17:6; Judges 21:25).

If only they had heeded and followed God's *careful now's*.

KEY QUESTION TO DAILY STAND: What cautions from God can save you from spiritual trips and falls?

O love of God, how rich and pure!
How measureless and strong!
It shall forevermore endure—
the saints' and angels' song.

"The Love of God"
Frederick M. Lehman

Day 28

Undying Love

KEY VERSE: *Grace to all who love our Lord Jesus Christ with an undying love. Ephesians 6:24*

Kevin and I do not write each other letters very often. But when we do, we sign off the same way every time. *Devoted to you.* It is our signature sentiment.

Thirteen of the New Testament epistles are attributed to Paul. In ten of the letters, he mentions Jesus in his closing remarks, and in the other three, he signs off with a reference pertaining to grace. Today's key verse has both in the closing comment that Paul wrote to the *saints, the faithful in Christ Jesus* in Ephesus (Ephesians 1:1).

Many claim to love Jesus. And it is a good assertion. But the descriptive attached to love that Paul uses at the end of Ephesians, ought to have our attention.

Undying.

Other versions say incorruptible, true, forever, in sincerity, never-ending, will never die, perfect sincerity, and undecayingly. The original word *aphtharsia* means indestructibility, incorruptibility; hence, immortality. Personally, undecayingly has my attention.

As I typed the word, the familiar red squiggly line showed up. The auto-correct function suggested I change it to unwearyingly, unceasingly, or unbecomingly. The only option that comes close is unceasingly, but it still does not have the same intent or assertion as *undecayingly*.

When something ceases, it stops or discontinues. But decay is decomposition, deterioration, and rot. A decaying tooth causes pain, infection, and loss. Decomposing garbage disintegrates. When something is neglected or damaged, it deteriorates or falls apart.

Agape love keeps on. It loves without end. That is

why our love relationship with God is a covenant love—it is eternal and continues to grow. Oh, we can stop showing our love to Him through our sinful choices, but when we are keeping to the covenant love we have in Jesus—when we are tucked in tight, abiding in and faithfully following our Lord, that love will never die, decay, deteriorate, or decompose.

KEY QUESTION TO DAILY STAND: Today, how will your actions show you love Jesus with an undeniably undying love?

Day 29

There is Where It is At

KEY VERSE: *...the children...will inherit it, and those who love his name will dwell there. Psalm 69:36*

There is a peculiar place. Countless times, we have been driving along some beautiful scenery on an interstate and I will exclaim, "Hey, Kev, look over there!" The man is driving 70-75 miles per hour, and I expect that he would know where *there* is.

Normally, when I assert *there*, Kevin's response is, "Where?"

At times I even complicate it further. "It is beautiful!" or "Can you believe it?"

The *there* and *it* do not give clear direction. However, thinking back, most of the time Kevin is aware of where *there* is and what I meant by *it*.

In today's key verse, we have an *it* and a *there*. And they reference the same thing: Zion.

It was referred to as God's holy hill, Jerusalem. The place where His temple was built, and where God's presence was thought to dwell, and where people worshiped, made sacrifice and brought offerings. Jerusalem was the main city in Judah. Bethlehem is in Judah. Jesus was born in Bethlehem.

The Psalmist says for those who love God's name, there is where it is at—*it* is what they will inherit and *there* is where they will dwell. The church of Jesus Christ is the people of God who love His name. For those who love His name, eternal life is what we inherit. Our destiny is to spend eternity with Jesus!

Since the Church began it has grown and spread across the globe. People on every continent belong to the same Church—it is *there* where Jesus is at! Not in a building or structure, but rather, in the hearts of those who love Him and His name. And it is there—at His name—where every knee will bow and every tongue will confess that Jesus Christ is Lord (Isaiah 45:23; Philippians 2:10-11).

Loving God bows to His will and bends a knee to Jesus. Dwell there: bowed to the lordship of Jesus Christ; worshiping, adoring, praising, and loving His name. It is there where we find peace, contentment, joy, hope, strength, and perseverance to love God faithfully and completely.

KEY POINT TO DAILY STAND: As we dwell *there*, we can declare, "It is well with my soul."

Day 30

Straight or Crooked Paths?

KEY VERSE: *...the Lord loves the righteous. Psalm 146:8*

Any connection, interaction, or inclination we have regarding God is always first initiated by Him. We cannot live right or make the right decisions without His Spirit wooing or moving us to righteousness.

This week my husband had the opportunity to pray with a woman named Ruby and lead her into a relationship with the Lord. She no longer needs to question her eternal home; it is secure because she repented of her sin, asked God to forgive her, and invited Jesus into her heart. At 89, Ruby does not have many years ahead of her, but like all of us who follow Jesus, her joy is complete.

At the end of Psalm 146:8, the Psalmist states the Lord loves the righteous. That is straightforward and concise. But before and after he wrote about who the Lord loves, the writer also declares what God does:

- Remains faithful forever (Psalm 146:6).
- Upholds the cause of the oppressed (Psalm 146:7).
- Gives food to the hungry (Psalm 146:7).
- Sets prisoners free (Psalm 146:7).
- Gives sight to the blind (Psalm 146:8).
- Lifts those who are bowed down (Psalm 146:8).
- Watches over the alien (Psalm 146:9).
- Sustains the fatherless and the widow (Psalm 146:9).

We can read this literally, or we can ask and allow the Holy Spirit to reveal the spiritual elements for each bullet point, which have lasting influence and effect on all those who love God. Take *he gives food to the hungry* as an example. For those who hunger and thirst for righteousness, Jesus promises they will be filled (Matthew 5:6).

Or *sets prisoners* free. Chains are not only for felons and law breakers. Many followers of Jesus are bound to the past, chained to an old habit or hang-up, linked to unhealthy relationships, or shackled by heavy burdens. The Psalmist declares those who hope in the Lord (Psalm 146:5), who praise the Lord (Psalm 146:1-2), and who do not trust in mortal men (Psalm 146:3) can be set free, upheld, given understanding, lifted, watched over, and sustained.

On the other hand He frustrates the ways of the wicked (Psalm 146:9). Their sin is the path they chose and is against God; therefore, He makes their journey crooked and bent.

For those who said yes to Jesus at a younger age than Ruby, we have more opportunity to see God at work, to witness the change He brings to a life, to experience His healing and provision, and to tell others all about it!

To those who wholeheartedly trust the Lord, who do not lean on their own understanding, and acknowledge Him in all their ways, God promises straight paths (Proverbs 3:5-6).

Loving God chooses the way to straight paths. Those people are righteous, and God loves them.

KEY POINT TO DAILY STAND: Fearing God loves God. Loving God trusts God. Trusting God lives right. Living right fears God.

> "O Lord, God of heaven,
> the great and awesome God,
> who keeps his covenant of love
> with those who love him
> and obey his commands..."
>
> Nehemiah 1:5

BOOK 3
STAND daily
Observing God's Commands

"And now, O Israel, what does the Lord require of you but to fear the Lord…to observe God's commands…"
Deuteronomy 10:12-13

Throughout the next thirty days, each daily reading will focus on a verse from Psalm 119.

Each day's reading is set up in the same manner:

- Title
- Key Verse
- Key Content
- Key Point

These daily readings are designed to encourage you to grow, challenge you to change, and influence you to live as Jesus intends:

SLOW

Day 1

Be a Seeker

KEY VERSE: *Blessed are they who keep his statutes and seek him with all their heart. Psalm 119:2*

In my early teens my family rented a cabin on a lake. Near the resort there were many other kids to hang out with, and every night we played kick-the-can. The one who was *it* manned the can while everyone else scattered and hid. The seeker pursued and tagged the hiders who then became frozen near the can while the hiders attempted to lure the seeker away from the can. Should a hider kick the can without being tagged, the frozen ones were freed.

One night as I was hiding, I saw an opportunity to kick the can, but that plan was thwarted as the seeker came running around the corner of my hiding place. I took off squealing and laughing at full speed and was immediately stopped in my tracks by a clothesline across my opened mouth. For days the rope burn looked like I had jelly smeared across my cheeks at an odd angle.

The boy chasing me was running full tilt, but that is the way of a seeker—they must be all-in. To fully observe God's commands, according to today's key verse, we must seek Him with all our hearts.

The smaller words make a big difference. As we read God's Word, followers of Jesus must be careful and prudent to catch every word. The order and context are vital to our understanding. In Psalm 119:2, if we exchanged *them* for *Him*, then we would be seeking the commands instead of the Commander.

We can only observe what the Spirit of God reveals. If we only seek the commands, we will be incapable of keeping them. We need the Lord! We need His Spirit to enable us to observe what He reveals. As we seek Him, we observe His commands. However, remember, seekers are expected to be all in.

Deuteronomy 10:12-13 says we fear the Lord when we observe His commands. The word observe means to keep, guard, and watch. Therefore, we cannot view His commands from an observation deck. They are not meant to only be noticed; God intends we observe and obey His commands. And that takes seeking Him with a wholehearted pursuit.

As we seek God with all our hearts, He reveals His statutes, precepts, and commands. As we truly seek Him, a desire to know Him and His will embeds deep within our souls. Followers of Jesus who observe God's commands should also choose them as their lifestyle and mindset. But that requires being all-in as we seek Him.

KEY POINT TO DAILY STAND: We cannot faithfully observe God's commands from an observation deck.

Day 2

Consideration

KEY VERSE: *I would not be put to shame when I consider all your commands. Psalm 119:6*

Kevin and I have been parenting for thirty-three straight years. In a few short months, our job will be finished, as the youngest of our six children turns eighteen. That does not mean we kick them to the curb, but it does mean as parents, though we are willing to continue to guide and give wisdom, we no longer offer our opinion unless it is asked of us.

In all humbleness if they choose a harmful path or choose to turn away from the Lord, it will not be because we spiritually failed them or neglected to point them to Jesus.

We were intentional to parent them well—with a Biblical perspective. We are not perfect, but we desired to do right. We had a responsibility to the Lord. He entrusted our children to us, and we chose to raise them to know Jesus and to trust God's Word as their foundation.

Throughout the past thirty-three years, we never used the word *command* in our parenting:

- Honey, I *command* you to clean your room!
- Son, I *command* that you stop yelling at your brother!
- Hey, you know using your cell phone at the table goes against our family *commandments*!
- The next time you choose this behavior or attitude, perhaps you should consider our *commands*!

No! That was not how we wanted to instill obedience

or respect. But God does. And it is good! Because everything He does is good (James 1:17). Giving us His commands and expecting us to follow and adhere to them is good. To live well and right, we need His commands!

I looked up Psalm 119:6 in thirty-five versions of the Bible. In only a couple the two phrases that make up the verse were swapped; however, in each edition, *I would never be put to shame* begins with the same word:

Then.

It is an important word. Then why is it omitted from today's key verse? For emphasis and to point to significance! Omitting *then* keeps our attention to the thought. But adding *then* implies we need to back the train up and make a connection.

Psalm 119:5 is the connector. "Oh, that my ways were steadfast in obeying your decrees!" And yet, this verse needs Psalm 119:4 attached to it. "You have laid down precepts that are to be fully obeyed." So, let us connect these three thoughts:

- God gives commands for us to obey…
- then we intentionally live them out…
- and when we do, we are not put to shame.

This means you can assuredly stand before God and pray and plead to Him with courage; boldly witness to others and confidently look yourself in the eye. In Matthew Henry's Complete Bible Commentary regarding Psalm 119:4-6, he concluded, "Those that are upright may take the comfort of their uprightness."

KEY QUESTION TO DAILY STAND: Feeling shame? Then, consider when was the last time you considered considering all of God's commands?

Day 3

Stay, Never Stray

KEY VERSE: *I seek you with all my heart; do not let me stray from your commands. Psalm 119:10*

STAND unmasked is the fourth book in the STAND series. *Wander well in the wilderness* is the subtitle for the Bible study based in Exodus. It highlights the Israelites who wandered in the wilderness, but the wandering was not the problem—their straying was. We are no different. Like the old hymn, "Come, Thou Fount of Every Blessing" states, "…prone to wander…prone to leave the God I love."

God never calls us to stray, but He may allow us to wander in the wilderness. How we wander matters, as it can be a purposeful time filled with significant spiritual lessons. But because straying is not an assignment from God, it will never spiritually benefit us. It is possible to wander well and remain tucked in tight to Jesus. But when we stray, we drift.

Hebrews 2:1 says, "We must pay careful attention, therefore, to what we have heard, so that we do not drift away." In this verse the original word for *drift* means to glide past or to personally fall away from duty.

When God assigns a wilderness, He intends that we will grow deeper roots and trust Him more. When we drift away or stray, we glide past the truth that guides and protects, and we neglect or forget the commands that keep us steady, rooted on a firm foundation, and standing on solid ground.

The Psalmist tells us how to tuck in tight, so we do not stray and leave the God we love: seek Him with all our hearts. Yes, throughout the four volumes of *STAND daily*, because it is a consistent command in God's Word, wholeheartedly seeking God is a recurring theme.

It makes zero sense that we would receive all God's

blessing and the benefits of His promises if we have drifted away from His commands. When we stray we become spiritually fainthearted, halfhearted, or coldhearted. It is audacious and insolent to claim we know and follow Jesus yet position our wants and wishes before God's commands. And then when we stray, we wonder why: often leaving us doubting God, presuming upon His promises, or assuming He went silent. When in fact we drifted away or strayed from God's commands.

Getting back on your spiritual track requires seeking the Lord with all your heart. Read and study His Word; get on your knees in prayer; regularly worship; serve others. And observe all God's commands—it is how we know true contentment and experience real pleasure—no matter what!

KEY POINT TO DAILY STAND: A slow fade will have us stray, but SLOW livin' has us staying tucked in tight to Jesus and living as He intends.

Day 4

Sin-seared or Sincere?

KEY VERSE: *I have hidden your word in my heart…Psalm 119:11*

Applied to the brain osmosis is a subtle or gradual process of unconscious assimilation of ideas, knowledge, and know-how. I recently saw a picture of a student's head sandwiched between a stack of books. It is silly to think that if the book remained attached to her head, she would know and understand the contents by osmosis.

Similarly, if our Bibles remain unopened and unread, how can we observe God's commands?

Bible apps are convenient, but they are also a detriment to spiritual growth. They come in handy in waiting rooms and at coffee shops, or as we are stalled in a long line at the grocery store, or in the parking lot waiting for our kids, and for those who have trouble reading the written word.

The same app we sometimes rely on can also be a disadvantage. When the pastor invites everyone to open their Bibles, the sound of ruffling paper from many pages turning is like the sweet sound of a musical offering to the Lord. Using a Bible app while God's Word is preached or studied comes with distraction. Unless all notifications and potential pop-up announcements are turned off, they can squelch a message that God has for us.

As we read, study, memorize, and apply God's Word in our life, imagine the treasure-trove of help, guidance, and protection of His commands when sin knocks at our door. Envision the deactivation, disarmament, and disabling from the strongholds of worry, fear, anxiety, bitterness, envy, hatred, and unforgiveness. Consider the nuggets of truth that can be embedded in the nooks and crannies of our souls and used when needed at the exact moment we are weary, weak, or worn out.

Sin sears our hearts, making us hardened and calloused to God's will and His way. The apostle Paul cautions Timothy, "The Spirit clearly says that in later times some will abandon the faith and follow deceiving spirits and things taught by demons. Such teachings come through hypocritical liars whose consciences have been seared as with a hot iron" (1 Timothy 4:1-2). A sin-seared heart is incapable of being sincere.

The Psalmist knew how to keep his heart from being seared by sin. Psalm 119:11 reveals he opened his heart as a hiding place and hid God's Word there! He treasured God's Word in his mind; his will; his inner self.

We can only hide God's Word in our hearts if we read God's Word.

Go ahead—put the device down, get your Bible, and flip through the pages. But before you do, ask the Lord to open the eyes of your heart to see what His Spirit wants to reveal. Hiding His Word will not happen by osmosis, nor by education. God's Word gets into our hearts by His revelation!

KEY CHALLENGE TO DAILY STAND: Be sincere and hide God's Word in your heart—it will keep you from being seared by sin.

Day 5

Stranger Things

KEY VERSE: *I am a stranger on earth; do not hide your commands from me…Psalm 119:19*

Inheritance is a blessing for some, but a curse for others. It is a sad day when elderly parents pass away. But it is ridiculous how quickly some siblings grow claws and fangs when the inheritance is divided and allocated. It happens when adult children assume their parent's hard-earned money becomes their birthright. In some cultures that might be true, but it would behoove more sibling groups to view inheritance as a gift, not a right.

The children of God have an inheritance. 1 Peter 1:3-4 says, "…in [God's] great mercy he has given us new birth…through the resurrection of Jesus…and into an inheritance that can never perish, spoil, or fade—kept in heaven for you…" If we are in a relationship with God through Jesus, this inheritance is promised for us!

At salvation our eternal home is secure. Though we live on earth, heaven is our home. We belong there. We are sojourners here—just passing through until God calls us home. Nothing on earth will completely satisfy us. Everything is temporary. When we breathe our last breath here, we go home empty-handed. When we meet Jesus face-to-face, if we are holding an earthly inheritance, how can our Savior take hold of our hand?

In the key verse, the word stranger can be replaced with *sojourner*. The original word means a temporary dweller or a newcomer who has no inherited rights. Oh, that we would take our eyes off what we think we deserve, off what we believe is not fair, off what others have, and off ourselves, so that we can intentionally observe God's commands.

In the bookend verses of Psalm 119:19, the Psalmist pleads for God to open eyes to see wonderful things in His law (Psalm 119:18), and claims his soul is consumed with longing for God's laws at all times (Psalm 119:20).

Opened eyes and consumed souls are prepared to observe God's commands.

Distracted followers cannot discern God's will, nor His way. Sojourners do not aimlessly wander; they are well aware of where home is, but they are also willing to wander well until they are welcomed home to enjoy their inheritance of eternity with Jesus.

KEY POINT TO DAILY STAND: The danger to being a stranger on earth, is to ignore or neglect God's commands.

Day 6
Arrogance Consequence

KEY VERSE: *You rebuke the arrogant, who are cursed and who stray from your commands. Psalm 119:21*

Arrogance may be one of the ugliest traits people can exhibit. It is often hidden by a mask of confidence and poise. But behind the façade is egotism, pride, and insolence. Arrogant people tend to manipulate, deflect responsibility or blame, and they need to be right. They brag and exaggerate their accomplishments and abilities. Their ideas are always the best and will get done their way. Arrogant people will not negotiate, and because they are ultra-competitive, they will seek to push their agendas ahead even if it means stepping on or in front of another, especially if that one is a threat to their success.

How can an arrogant Christian remain tucked in tight to Jesus? Arrogance is prideful; surrender requires humbleness. Arrogance is resistant; abiding in Jesus requires submitting to Him. Arrogance has eyes on self; followers of Jesus are urged to fix our eyes on Him.

There are times God's Word has a hard word for us. Today is such a time. Let us look at the key verse in three parts:

- Who stray from your commands
- Who are cursed
- You rebuke the arrogant

First, on Day 3 of Observe God's Commands the focus was to stay tucked in tight to Jesus so that we do not stray from God's commands. Today the Psalmist tells us the arrogant stray and drift away.

Next, we read that the arrogant are cursed. What does that mean? Arrogant folks think they set the standard and expect others to live by it. But those who claim to follow God must also observe His commands, otherwise their ways compete with His. God is not our competitor; He is our Commander. When we allow pride to gain any ground in our lives, arrogance becomes a stronghold in our souls. And the slippery slope of spiritual decline begins.

Proverbs 2:6 says, "For the Lord gives wisdom…" And Proverbs 8:13 says, "To fear the Lord is to hate evil; I hate pride and arrogance…" Solomon took literary freedom and personified wisdom, communicating wisdom and arrogance cannot coexist. Those who choose arrogance over God's commands are cursed. Covenant protects and provides. Arrogance allows calamity and destruction.

Finally, God is not silent on the topic of arrogance. With stern disapproval He rebukes and reproves it. When necessary God will chide His children—He will express His disapproval. There is purpose when God reveals arrogance in our hearts. It gives us an opportunity to humble ourselves and repent.

We have a choice: observe God's commands or suffer whatever curse comes. Before we deem God unloving, unfair, or unreasonable, perhaps that is a good time to allow Him access to check for arrogance deep within.

KEY THOUGHT TO DAILY STAND: Avoid arrogance; it is blinded to God's Commands.

Day 7

A Clean Sweep

KEY VERSE: *...strengthen me according to your word.* **Psalm 119:28**

    Melting marshmallows or over-melting butter, especially in a microwave, is messy. Eating an ice cream cone in the sun on a hot summer day will also cause a melting mess. Though things melt, they remain stuck, and a clean-up effort is necessary.
    In the *Wizard of Oz* the Wicked Witch melted when Dorothy doused her with a bucket of water. But she remained on the floor in what looked like a pile of brown sugar. Then the girl took another bucket of water and poured it over the mess and swept it out the door.
    The mess left by the melted witch was a reminder of what previously had the girl weary, weak, and worn out. Leaving the pile, leaves the mess. Therefore, Dorothy carried out a clean sweep.
    In the King James Version, Psalm 119:28 begins, "My soul melteth for heaviness…" The word *melteth* means to drop through, leak, pour out, or melt. The idiom *my heart sank* means to lose hope, grieve, be despaired, upset, or regretful.
    When we are weary, weak, and worn out, our souls become heavy, and they leak. Condolences, concerns, and care from people may help, but they will never plug leaks in our souls. We need to be doused with holy water!
    This water does not come in liquid form; it comes by way of the Holy Spirit. God's Word soothes, quenches, and satisfies. It seals the leaks and strengthens our souls. His Word calms our fears and leads us on paths of righteousness.
    Leaks in our soul reveal we misunderstand or misinterpret burden-bearing. Jesus said, "My yoke is easy

and my burden is light" (Matthew 11:30). We are not made to wear heaviness, but we are called to bear burdens. The burden itself does not need to be heavy; the heaviness comes when we try to bear it alone on our own strength.

"Come to me, all you who are weary and burdened, and I will give you rest" (Matthew 11:28). If we observe this command of Jesus, we will bear burdens without soul leakage. He gives further direction and charges us to take His yoke upon us and learn from Him. When we do as He commands, we will find rest for our wearied and worried souls (Matthew 11:29).

KEY POINTS TO DAILY STAND: Melted souls leak. Heavy souls are weak. God's Word mends leakage, restores weakness, and strengthens souls.

Day 8

Off Track

KEY VERSE: *I run in the path of your command...Psalm 119:32*

All four of my boys were a part of the cross-country team in high school. Two ran to improve endurance and positively affect their upcoming basketball season, while another ran because it kept him active. But for one, it was his main sport that he excelled in.

Prior to a race, to get familiar with the course, all teams walk or jog the path. One time we were at a large park on the shores of Lake Huron where many schools were competing in one race. That year the girls ran before the boys. Shortly after the girl's race began, the front runner took a wrong turn and each participant followed. Consequently, every runner was disqualified.

After their disqualification, the girls' coaches had questions.

"What were you thinking?"

"How did this happen?"

"Don't you remember the right path?"

Each coach corrected their team on what to do should it happen again.

In his letter to the churches in Galatia, it might appear Paul commends the Galatians as he says, "You were running a good race" (Galatians 5:7a). However, remember the little words make a big difference. Notice the tense; it says *were*, not *are*. Paul was being corrective, not offering commendation.

After his initial comment Paul's correction came as a question. "Who cut in on you and kept you from obeying..." (Galatians 5:7b). Being confronted with questions helps us understand how we spiritually got off track:

- What roadblock hindered your walk of faith?
- What obstacle impeded you?
- What or who interrupted you from living as Jesus intends?
- Who or what interrupted your firm stance on your path of righteousness?

Are these questions to make us feel guilty or questions to correct our missteps? If we follow someone down the wrong path, we cannot fully observe God's commands. Likewise, if we choose a wrong turn, we avoid and neglect to observe them, as well.

Recently, I was in a corrective conversation with a teen. I told her she was at a crossroads—one way went the right way, the other led to nowhere good. Which path she took was her choice. I reminded the young lady what missionary/pastor/author E. Stanley Jones once said, "You can make your choices, but you cannot choose the consequences."

We are all in the same race—headed somewhere in this life. We are either running in the path of God's commands or turning away from them. How we run is our choice; where we land is not. Therefore, we ought to observe God's commands and choose His paths of righteousness.

KEY QUESTION TO DAILY STAND: Are you spiritually off-track? If so, how did it happen and will you welcome God's correction?

Day 9

Delighted

KEY VERSE: *Direct me in the path of your commands, for there I find delight. Psalm 119:35*

As a mom I cannot recall a time one of my kids responded, "I would be delighted to," when I asked them to do something they really did not want to do. I am no different.

For seven years a good friendship went silent. Some say our friendship broke up. But last summer God made it abundantly clear I was to make the first move so He could mend the relationship. My response? "I would be delighted to!"

NOT!

My reply was, "Uh-uh! No way, Lord!" This occurred days before I was going to teach a Bible study at a week-long family camp. His reply to me? "Then how can I use you to teach others if you are unwilling to obey Me?"

OUCH!

"Ok, Lord, I will do it."

But I still did not view it as a delight. That came after the step of obedience when my friend welcomed me to her campsite, and we talked for close to an hour. What needed to be said was said. Apologies were made, forgiveness extended, and what once was dormant came to life. A friendship was resurrected, restored, and renewed! Oh, what a delight it is!

Along paths of righteousness we are called to obey. But we cannot obey what we do not observe. For seven long years I missed my friend. I had already forgiven any wrongdoing or misunderstanding, so the command to forgive was settled. But when God called me to initiate, my stubbornness and self-righteousness reared up and I was far from *delight* over that command.

SLOW livin' is not about comfort or having our rights heard and met. Serving God, Loving God, Observing His Commands, and Walking in all His ways is about fearing God. I was more afraid of the consequences of disobeying the command than I was at initiating a face-to-face encounter with my friend.

Too many followers of Jesus look for pleasure and satisfaction first. But we are called to observe His commands and follow them. It is not up to us to find delight and then follow God's commands. Rather, His commands are for us to first observe and follow. And when we do His direction brings delight.

KEY POINT TO DAILY STAND: When we take direction from God, we take pleasure in His commands.

Day 10

Truth

KEY VERSE: *Do not snatch the word of truth from my mouth, for I have put my hope in your laws. Psalm 119:43*

It is unknown who to credit for the idiom "You took the words right out of my mouth!" If we imagine this literally, it makes for a humorous picture.

But even if we voice the same thoughts as another, it is possible they are untrue. That is because we are fallible; however, God is infallible.

There are many debates within Christian culture. The ones that are preferential are not worrisome. How we receive Holy Communion is one example. Some prefer to kneel at an altar rail, others would like to remain in their seats, and there are those who choose intinction as their mode of partaking in the body and blood of Jesus. Preferences should not divide because there is common ground at the core of the inclination.

When opinion trumps truth schism and factions develop. God's children are not meant to live in discord, but it happens when the words tumbling out of our mouths do not line up with the truth of God's Word.

We can trust in God's commands, statutes, and precepts, if we place our hope in His laws. This *hope* is a wait. Perhaps opinion is birthed when Christians are not willing to wait for God to formulate His truth in their hearts; therefore, they lean on their own understanding and acknowledge their thoughts, disregarding His Word.

The truth is that all of God's Word is the whole truth and nothing but the truth. The authority of Scripture is at the base of the debates that divide.

In 2 Kings 22, King Josiah did what was right in the eyes of the Lord, not turning aside to the right or to the left.

The king sent his secretary on a business trip to the temple. While there, the high priest told the secretary, "I have found the Book of the Law…" (2 Kings 22:8). When the secretary reported the finding to the king he said, "…the high priest has given me a book…" and then he read from it in the presence of the king (2 Kings 22:10).

Again, the little words make a great impact. And in this case, a capitalized *B* does too. The priest found *the* Book, but the secretary reported about *a* book. 2 Kings 22:11 records the king's response. "When the king heard the words of the Book of the Law, he tore his robes."

Then he sent his secretary on a mission to inquire about all that is written in the Book stating, "…our fathers have not obeyed the words…they have not acted in accordance with all that is written there…" (2 Kings 22:13).

The words had been snatched out of their mouths because they were not planted in their hearts. They stopped putting their hope in the Lord and His law, and it had dire consequences.

KEY POINT TO DAILY STAND: Truth gets revealed by the Spirit of God, it does not get revised by manmade thoughts or opinions.

Day 11

Love Connection

KEY VERSE: *...for I delight in your commands because I love them. Psalm 119:47*

In *Serve God*, the first book of this series, Day 18 is titled, "Conjunction Connection." The function of a conjunction is to connect words, phrases, clauses, and sentences. The first word in today's key verse is a conjunction.

Psalm 119:44-46 has four *I will* statements that connect to the key verse:

- I will always obey your law.
- I will walk about in freedom.
- I will speak of your statutes.
- I will not be put to shame.

1. **Always obey.** The original word for always means continuity—it goes on every day without interruption. As if the Psalmist wanted to make sure his intent was clear, he added, "...forever and ever." The first *forever* means it continues through his life. The additional *and ever* means perpetuity—his obedience is endless, going into eternity.
2. **Walk about.** It means to live. The Psalmist declared that because he sought out (he observed) God's precepts, he was free to live—not doing as he wanted; rather, living within the confines of God's commands, and that brought freedom to his life. It seems paradoxical, but it is the truth! Holy statutes freed him to live within the limits of God's laws.

3. **Speak of.** We must be intentional to declare God's commands and testify how they apply to our life. The Psalmist was willing to tell anyone, even kings, about the affect God's commands had on him. The message for us is to be bold; be courageous; be strong! And be willing to tell others about the Lord's commands.
4. **Unashamed.** There is no room for timidity, shyness, or cowardice in kingdom work. God's commands free, protect, and convict us; they challenge and keep us; they influence, inspire, and impact us. They also teach, correct, rebuke, and train us up in righteousness (2 Timothy 3:16). It is a privilege and honor to stand for the Lord and tell of His goodness and greatness!

The Psalmist declares the *I will's* because he delights in and loves God's commands. Love is the connector!

As we love God's Word, plus His will and His ways, we will be inclined to conform to them. And it will be our delight to convey and converse about His ways.

KEY CHALLENGE TO DAILY STAND: Make a love connection with God's Commands today!

Day 12

Hands and Knees

KEY VERSE: *I lift my hands to your commands, which I love, and I meditate on your decrees. Psalm 119:48*

When I was a little girl, my older sister and I loved our ritual just before bedtime. Our dad would get on his hands and knees and give us *horsey rides* down the hall to our bedroom. When Kevin and I were first married, we rented that small ranch-style house from my parents. It took an adult perspective to realize that every ride on my father's back meant his hands and knees were on the hardwood floor. How deep was our father's love!

In the Old Testament there is more than one Hebrew word for *hand*. In today's key verse the original word is *kaf*, which is pronounced how a Brit would say calf. Used one hundred and eighty times in the Old Testament, the Hebrew word means the palm, hollow, or flat part of the hand.

The Psalmist says he lifts his hands to God's commands and meditates on His decrees (Psalm 119:48). The great commentator, Matthew Henry, pointed out to raise our hands to God's commands is, "…not only to praise it, but practice it."

In some churches it is common to see people raise their hands as they worship through song. Simply put, the representation of palms facing forward portrays adoration and praise. It is also a sign of reverence to the majesty and might, and the strength and honor of the Lord. When palms are lifted upward it suggests submission. But it can also mean acceptance and an indication of receiving the things of the Lord. Hands lifted forward or palms up, are both symbolic of surrender.

Outward signs are not absolute indicators of a heart of worship. We must be mindful that all acts of worship are conceived within; therefore, those who do not raise hands may still worship Jesus if He is foremost on their minds and in their hearts. It is also possible that there may be one in the sanctuary with a raised hand, yet worship is not on their mind or in their heart.

Our hands can both praise and practice, but it is more a matter of the heart. Lifted hands denote we need God's strength for whatever the task, wherever the call.

A bended knee conveys meditation of decrees. Similar to keeping our hands at our side while worshiping, we can also stand tall and still bend a knee because it is also conceived within.

It is the way of a follower of Jesus to be heedful to raise hands to God's commands and diligent to bend a knee to His decrees—because we love Him and His Word.

KEY QUESTION TO DAILY STAND: Do you observe God's commands with hands and knees?

Day 13

Dillydally or Dawdle

KEY VERSE: *I will hasten and not delay to obey your commands. Psalm 119:60*

Dillydally is a fun word to say. A true grammar-buff would know *dillydally* is an example of reduplication—where the meaning of a word is expressed through repeating parts of a word. *Dawdle* is another fun word. Both mean the same thing: to waste time.

Hasten is their antonym.

Ask any of my six kids what the Harbin Family Motto is, and without delay, they will say, "Later never happens." Kevin and I did not raise our kids in a militant manner, but there are just some things that require immediacy. God's commands modeled the mindset for us:

- Forgive (Matthew 6:14-15).
- Get along (Psalm 133:1).
- Apologize (James 5:16).
- Read the Bible (Joshua 1:8).
- Pray (1 Thessalonians 5:17).
- Do not worry (Matthew 6:25).

The Bible is chock full of commands we are to obey without delay. The Psalmist leads by example. He says, "I will hasten to obey."

In the late 1800s a Civil War veteran turned evangelist, adapted words from an anonymous writer into lyrics of the hymn, "Have You Any Room for Jesus."

The chorus says:

Room for Jesus, King of Glory!
Hasten now, His word obey!

Swing the heart's door widely open!
Bid Him enter while you may.

God's Word will encourage us, and His commands will challenge us. Observing for the sake of knowledge is not enough. Obedience is our duty, honor, privilege, and joy. It is why loving His commands is vital—we do not avoid or ignore or neglect what we love. We hasten to what is important, meaningful, necessary, and life-giving.

Many things in life require taking time to accomplish: career change, furthering education, saving for a mortgage, or planning for retirement. But when it comes to our relationship with Jesus, we must bid Him to enter the doors He is knocking on.

We especially need to make room for Jesus in the secret places of our hearts. Dillydallying and dawdling to welcome Him in, has unforeseen outcomes that impede our walk with Jesus; therefore, make haste!

KEY POINT TO DAILY STAND: Do not delay; obey His commands! After all, later never happens.

Day 14

I Believe

KEY VERSE: *Teach me knowledge and good judgment, for I believe in your commands. Psalm 119:66*

    I grew up in a church where we corporately declared the Apostles' Creed every Sunday. This Creed has three *I believe* statements; each is followed with supporting points. I still have the article of faith memorized. Declarations and articulated words are pointless if they only flow from memory and are not conceived in the heart.

    My dad modeled how to recite the Creed. As a child I watched in wonder; as a teen I was mortified and embarrassed; as a young adult I had respect and regard for his demonstrative enthusiasm as he declared what he believed. Dad's personality is shy, but his willingness to take a stand for Jesus is bold, confident, and fearless. In that full sanctuary there was no doubt what my dad, Allen Schweizer, believed!

    According to Psalm 119:66, observing God's commands is a prerequisite to knowing God's understanding and wisdom, plus distinguishing God's judgment—His discretion and discernment. Overt characterization is not a prerequisite, nor is it conditional on sharing or declaring our beliefs. But what is necessary is determining if our beliefs are reserved for times of worship, are only on our minds, or if they are foundational to every aspect of our life.

    Our beliefs can bring structure to our life. They should affect our decisions, behaviors, feelings, relationships, and reactions. And they ought to be lived out every day.

    We must take note of two things in today's key verse. First, notice the conjunction *for*. Learning and exercising God's knowledge and His judgment connects to believing in

His commands.

Next, do not miss the little word that makes a big difference!

In!

If we removed it the phrase would read *I believe your commands*. Believing them is knowledge—accepting they simply belong to God and each one stands alone. However, believing *in* God's commands stands firm on all of them *and* collectively trusts in them to teach, correct, rebuke, and train us up in righteousness.

When we believe in His commands, we observe them to guide and protect; encourage and challenge; convict and comfort; teach and preach; evangelize and disciple. They offer wisdom, insight, assistance, and understanding. They reveal alternative choices to what the world has to offer. They set us straight and reposition our perspective. They accompany us through hardship and attend us in crisis.

As His children, we need His commands!

KEY QUESTION TO DAILY STAND: Do you believe God's commands, or do you believe *in* them?

The Apostle's Creed

I believe in God, the Father Almighty,
maker of heaven and earth;

And in Jesus Christ
his only Son, our Lord;
who was conceived by the Holy Spirit,
born of the Virgin Mary,
suffered under Pontius Pilate,
was crucified, dead, and buried;
the third day he rose from the dead;

he ascended into heaven,
and sitteth at the right hand
of God the Father Almighty;
from thence he shall come to judge the
quick and the dead.

I believe in the Holy Spirit,
the holy catholic church,
the communion of saints,
the forgiveness of sins,
the resurrection of the body,
and the life everlasting.
Amen.

Day 15

Hindsight

KEY VERSE: *It was good for me to be afflicted so that I might learn your decrees. Psalm 119:71*

    Anyone who learns a valuable lesson agrees that hindsight is 20/20. A difficult decision in our past becomes easier in the future. Clarity over a situation comes after all the pieces fall into place from looking back. If we are willing to notice, it is after a difficult circumstance that we gain perspective, understanding, and recognition.

    Hindsight is invaluable to our faith journey. Just today a friend communicated to me about her painful and trying circumstances from the last few weeks. Immediately, I was struck with an awareness that could only come through the Holy Spirit. Looking back on the past few months gave perspective and clarity to her current situation. God allowed the past crisis to connect to the current hardship.

    Why?

    Before the question is answered another must be asked. Is God only present in good things?

    So why did God allow a past affliction to butt up to a current hardship? Psalm 119:71 has an answer. "…so that I might learn your decrees." Some afflictions are disciplines; others are assignments. Both come from our good Father.

    First, the Lord disciplines those He loves (Proverbs 3:12). Yet, affliction that comes through His correction, eventually produces a harvest of righteousness and peace…IF…if we choose to see it as a method of discipline so we become more Christlike (Hebrews 12:11).

    Next, afflictions as assignments. One crisis in my life was cancer. I did not volunteer for that trying time, but God made it abundantly clear He assigned it for His glory (Psalm 16:5). Much good came from that affliction. Negotiation was not acceptable; participation was the order. Falling to pieces was not the agenda; trusting in God's promises and learning his precepts was the mandate.

Hindsight from that affliction offers valuable lessons, unbelievable opportunities, powerful displays of God's providence, sturdy roots of faith, deeper insights into His Word, and so much more! When we view afflictions as interruptions, nuisances, inconvenience, or unacceptable predicaments, we miss the good God desires to bring into our life and the significance of observing His commands.

KEY CONSIDERATION TO DAILY STAND: E. Stanley Jones said, "Jesus did not bear the cross, He used it."

Day 16

Purpose

KEY VERSE: *Your hands made me and formed me; give me understanding to learn your commands. Psalm 119:73*

Oh, the quest for purpose! Too many people get bogged down by searching and wondering what their purpose is. Followers of Jesus do not need to look; we need to see what God says regarding *His* purpose for us.

Years ago, shortly after my husband was appointed as pastor to a particular church, I remember the song leader stood before the people saying how thankful he was that the solutions to 95% of our problems could be found in God's Word.

My husband could not let the people believe that was true! The pastor could not allow the falsity to stand. It was possible someone in that sanctuary thought, "What's the purpose in being here or reading the Bible since the solution to my issue obviously falls in the 5% category?"

Following the singing, Pastor Kevin stood before the people and corrected the man. He said something like, "A correction must be made. You will not find solutions to 95% of life's problems in the Bible. God covers 100% of our issues in His Word."

Throughout the Bible God reveals everything we need to know—He offers solutions to problems; He discloses how we manage relationships, how to handle money, how to fight right, and so much more to live as Jesus intends. He tells us what we must do and what we should avoid. He does not leave us in the dark on any topic!

We are individually made from His hands. He fashioned and formed us in the womb. Too many people get stuck questioning or regretting who the womb belonged to, and they disregard or overlook Who did the fashioning. To know our purpose, we must ignore the womb and pay attention to Whom it was that formed us there.

When we personally accept that God created us exactly as He deemed fit, then after we enter into a relationship with Him through His Son, Jesus, we can appreciate the good work He did in forming us. God accomplishes His good work through us (Philippians 2:13).

Oh, that we would realize we were made for SLOW livin'! We find purpose as we serve God, love God, observe His commands, and walk in all His ways.

KEY POINT TO DAILY STAND: He made you on purpose to live out His intended purposes.

Day 17

S.O.S.

KEY VERSE: *All your commands are trustworthy; help me...Psalm 119:86*

The universal code for distress is SOS. Contrary to opinion, it does not stand for *save our ship* or *save our souls*. SOS is derived from the code developed by Samuel Morse. Varying electric pulses were assigned to the letters of the alphabet and used to communicate messages. Three dots, followed by three dashes, and ending with three dots again is the coded cry for help.

Christians do not need a special code to petition the Lord for His help. We need faith and prayer: faith in the Sovereign Lord of the universe to help us in our time of need. And communication through prayer, whether they are silent pleas or cries of "Please, Lord," they call for His help.

Being familiar with God's commands directs our hope, brings comfort, points us in the right direction, steadies and preserves us. Even still, the rewards and benefits and value in observing His commands have no end:

- His mercies are new every morning!
- His grace is boundless!
- His promises never fail!
- His steadfast love never ceases!

And His commands are trustworthy! Therefore, as Psalm 119:86 says, we can call on Him for help. But the Psalmist was not talking about general help; his cry for help came because he was being persecuted without cause.

What do we do when we are being treated unfairly? How do we respond when we are deceived? What is our reaction when someone disappoints us? Where do we turn when betrayed?

The answer is the same to each question. "All your commands are trustworthy" (Psalm 119:86). Before his cry for help, the Psalmist made the declaration. It is imperative followers of Jesus read and study the Bible so we can become acquainted and familiar with God's commands.

KEY QUESTION TO DAILY STAND: If you fully trusted God's commands, how many cries for help would you take back?

Day 18

Eternal

KEY VERSE: *Your word, O Lord, is eternal; it stands firm in the heavens. Psalm 119:89*

Our finite minds cannot fully grasp eternity. Oh, we can understand the concept, but we have limits and eternity does not. A day is cut off after twenty-four hours, a month is no longer than thirty-one days, and a year is complete in twelve months. Limits are set because we need order. Without the boundary of time, chaos would erupt.

But without the hope and assurance of our eternal home, we would be in chaos. And yet, because of our inability to have an eternal mindset, we tend to think of eternity as something that *will* happen, when, by virtue of its definition, it has always been intact. Frankly, it has never ceased because eternity has no beginning nor end.

Jesus said, "I am the Alpha and the Omega…who is, and who was, and who is to come…" (Revelation 1:8). Alpha and omega are the first and last letters of the Greek alphabet. Like bookends, everything else is held in between. And yet, in our minds, we still see things on the other side of the bookends, indicating there is more to the picture.

Let us view the beginning and the end in a cyclical fashion. As I type this, I can see my wedding ring glistening. When Kevin placed the ring on my finger thirty-four years ago, it came with a vow and declaration:

In token and pledge of our constant faith and abiding love,
with this ring I thee wed,
in the name of the Father, and of the Son,
and of the Holy Spirit.

When my husband performs a wedding ceremony,

prior to the man and woman exchanging rings, he holds them and mentions the shape: a circle symbolizing eternity. And since eternity has no end, neither should their love, so they should wear them in a conspicuous manner.

Not only are the three Persons of the Trinity eternal, but Psalm 199:89 declares that God's Word is also eternal; standing firm in the heavens. God is unchangeable and so is His Word! Throughout all time there is no proof of His Word varying or vacillating. Before He created the earth and everything in it, including man and woman, truth already existed. It has always been attached to God; therefore, it had no beginning, and it will have no end.

And because God is eternal and His Word is truth, it too is eternal. This ought to bring us joy and settle hope to the core of our souls. His commands set limits on our lives. They guide us to live holy and they teach us how to serve and love—Him and others. They correct us when we are wrong, and they set us on the path of righteousness.

They always have; always will!

KEY POINT TO DAILY STAND: The eternal Word of God stands firm; therefore, we ought to stand on it!

Day 19

Boundless

KEY VERSE: *...your commands are boundless.* **Psalm 119:96**

Recently, an acquaintance told me she disliked the word *boundaries*. It took me off guard because I appreciate the word. Even when she explained her position, I disagreed with the assessment. These are my words, not hers (frankly, her words were more descriptive as she took a defensive posture), but her issue was that boundaries hold her back and stifle her life.

It behooves us to not only perceive His commands as a mark of love from an eternal God but to also observe them as boundaries from a boundless God. It sounds paradoxical: a limitless God sets limits for His children.

Why? Because God knows we need them.

Throughout Psalm 119:81-96 the writer validates why we need them:

- Souls faint (v. 81).
- Eyes fail (v. 82).
- Impatience hinders (v. 84).
- Pitfalls await (v. 85).
- Persecution happens (v. 86).
- Destruction threatens (v. 95).

Before the Psalmist says God's commands are boundless, he says, "To all perfection I see a limit..." (Psalm 119:96). This world cannot satisfy our longing, nor can it fulfill our deepest needs. People are not able to love you most or know you best. Bank accounts, pension funds, or inheritances will not bring true contentment. Each one has its limits; none are boundless.

We have a longing to be captured by God's limitless love and a need to be protected by His boundless commands. God's love frees us to live well. His commands allow us to live right. Any Christian who feels stifled or held back by God's boundaries, needs to realign their thinking according to His Word and not their way.

Paul Gerhardt was a preacher in the 1600's. He married and had five children, of which four who died during childhood. Mr. Gerhardt also lost his wife while the surviving child was still young. Biographies agree he suffered through ministry and personal hardship, yet he penned more than 125 hymns.

In 1653 the good reverend penned the words to what later became the hymn, "Jesus, Thy Boundless Love to Me."

Jesus, your boundless love to me,
no thought can reach, no tongue declare;
Dwell in my heart eternally,
and reign without a rival there.
O Jesus, nothing may I do, but seek my joy in serving you.
O grant that nothing in my soul may dwell,
but your pure love alone;
Oh, may your love possess me whole,
my joy, my treasure, and my crown!
All coldness from my heart remove;
my every act, word, thought, be love.
This love unwearied I pursue,
and dauntlessly to you aspire;
Oh, may your love my hope renew,
burn in my soul like heavenly fire!
And day and night be all my care
to guard this sacred treasure there.
In suffering be your love my peace,
in weakness be your love my power;
and when the storms of life shall cease,
O Jesus, in that final hour,

be then my rod and staff and guide
and draw me safely to your side.

KEY POINT TO DAILY STAND: God's love knows no bounds and His commands are boundless.

> "When your words came,
> I ate them;
> they were my joy
> and my heart's delight,
> for I bear your name,
> O Lord God Almighty."
>
> Jeremiah 15:16

Day 20

Wiser Than

KEY VERSE: *Your commands make me wiser than my enemies...Psalm 119:98*

The old proverb *practice makes perfect* means if we diligently and persistently work at something we will improve on it. Just before David took down Goliath, he spoke to King Saul saying, "The Lord who delivered me from the paw of the lion and the paw of the bear will deliver me from the hand of this Philistine [Goliath]" (1 Samuel 14:37).

And right before he took the giant down, he stood up to Goliath and said, "I come against you in the name of the Lord Almighty...it is not by sword or by spear that the Lord saves; for the battle is the Lord's..." (1 Samuel 17:48).

Whether a lion or a bear was attacking his flock, or a nine-foot-tall giant was intimidating the whole Israelite army, David knew how to face his enemy. As a shepherd boy he was prepared to take down the animals because he was proficient with his slingshot. But he had zero practice on the battlefield, so he used what he knew.

David took God at His word. The teenager knew he was no match for a lion or a bear, let alone a giant! But He also trusted that the enemies he faced, furry or gigantic, were no match for the Lord Almighty!

God took down the giant, but He used David to do it. And because David was a willing warrior, God poured His wisdom into the young man, and David became wiser than the enemy.

1 Peter 5:8 is clear who our enemy is. "Your enemy the devil prowls around like a roaring lion looking for someone to devour." He looks for followers of Jesus he can deceive, distract, destroy, and ultimately, devour. He has

free reign in this world. He is permitted to badger, tempt, lure, and entice.

But we can be wiser than he because we belong to the Lord, and we have His commands. If we read them and claim them and trust them! Jeremiah 15:16 says when His words come to us, we ought to eat them. As we do we are overcome with His ways; His thoughts come to the forefront; His battle plan becomes our stratagem; His commands make us wiser than our enemy.

KEY CHALLENGE TO DAILY STAND: We have a choice: Be devoured by the enemy or devour the Word of God.

Day 21

Lamplight

KEY VERSE: *Your word is a lamp to my feet and a light for my path. Psalm 119:105*

A few weeks ago, after I had gone off to bed, Kevin fell asleep in our family room. He awoke shortly after and started to our bedroom. Groggy and unsteady, he lost his footing and tripped as he came through the threshold of the kitchen. The left side of his face struck a spindle of a kitchen chair.

Praise God he had glasses on as they saved his good eye! You see, my husband has extreme nearsightedness and twenty years ago he lost the center vision of his right eye. A spindle straight to the left eye would have put his vision in jeopardy. Though I slept through the mishap, I saw the blackened eye and bruised face first thing the next morning. Incidentally, though the small lamps we have on two small kitchen cabinets produce sufficient light, they would not have saved him from the trip and fall.

Back when Psalm 119:105 was written, people used different light sources. A lamp of sorts would be tied to a rope and swung out in front of a person to light the path ahead. At times, people would attach a lamp to their ankles to illume the way forward.

In Psalm 119:105, *feet* and *path* are metaphors to represent our walk of faith. The path metaphorically means our course of life. Throughout these daily readings, we have seen that God's commands direct and guide our life. But we must use the proper light source to maneuver the dark places and walk through the unknown terrain we face in life.

God's Word is different. To keep us standing firm in our faith, His Word sheds the light we need to shine His commands and truth into any darkened place of our mind or soul. It is good news that God provides the light source. If we keep His lamp burning and ever before us as we walk by faith, we do not have to grope around in darkness or wonder what our next step will be or where it will lead.

I wonder if our Bibles would shine literal light from their place on our nightstands, end tables, desks, backpacks, or carry-on bags if we would go to them more often. His Word is our beacon and promises to light our paths, but it will also guide us in thought and direct us in conversation. It will help us change course should we take a wrong turn.

Do not be deceived; though His Word will light the rocky paths through life, it may not rescue us from the difficult terrain. Some hard roads are designed and assigned by God. He promises to light our path and never leave us in the dark; He does not promise it will be smooth sailing.

KEY POINT TO DAILY STAND: To let our little light shine, we need the Word of God to light our path.

Day 22

For Keeps

KEY VERSE: *Away from me you evil doers, that I might keep the commands of God.* **Psalm 119:115**

When I was in elementary school, kids would gather in small circles in the dirt to play marbles. Someone would draw a circle with their finger, and then each participant would open their velvety pouches, select the amount agreed upon, and scatter the marbles within the circle. Each person flicked their shooter marble with their thumb into the circle attempting to knock their opponents' marbles out of the boundary marker.

Playing *for keeps* meant whatever marbles went outside the circle were kept by the one who made the shot. It is unclear which marble was worth more—cats-eye, steely, sunburst, swirly, just to name a few. It seemed it was subjective to the individual.

But life is not all fun and games. The Psalmist faced evildoers and double-minded men (Psalm 119:113; 115).

And so do we.

The commands of God are not subjective; they are objective. They are purposeful and meaningful; trustworthy and consistent; corrective and nourishing. God's ways are for keeps!

Double-minded folks are skeptical, halfhearted, and divided. Evildoers hurt others on purpose and look for mischief. They mentally and physically afflict, and they are socially and morally bad. How to deal with these types?

Keep God's commands. The evil and division from others will dissuade and distract us from the protection and guidance of God's Word.

The Psalmist says:

- You are my refuge (Psalm 119:114).
- You are my shield (Psalm 119:114).

The Psalmist pleads:

- Sustain me and I will live (Psalm 119:116).
- Do not let my hopes be dashed (Psalm 119:116).
- Uphold me and I will be delivered (Psalm 119:117).

The Psalmist declares:

- I love your law (Psalm 119:113).
- I have put my hope in your word (Psalm 119:114).
- I will always have regard for your decrees (Psalm 119:117).
- I love your statutes (Psalm 119:119).
- I stand in awe of your laws (Psalm 119:120).

The Psalmist warns:

- God rejects all who stray from His commands (Psalm 119:118).
- God discards the wicked (Psalm 119:119).

God is clear—He does not waver. He is not undecided. He is a keeper of His Word. Therefore, we should keep His commands and follow His ways…for keeps.

KEY THOUGHT TO DAILY STAND: What keepsakes are around that remind you to keep God's commands for keeps?

Day 23

Because

KEY VERSE: *Because I love your commands more than gold...and because I consider all your precepts right...Psalm 119:127-128*

Most parents of toddlers know to not begin a question with *why*. How come? Because the toddler will reply, "Because." And we all know when *because* is stand-alone, it is never a sufficient answer or useful response.

However, when used as a conjunction or preposition, it has great significance. In Psalm 119:127-128, *because* is used twice:

- Because I love your commands more than gold.
- Because I consider all your precepts right.

When we perceive God's commands from the vantage point of who He is rather than what His commands do for us, our spiritual roots will dive deep, and we will be more rooted in faith. Because when we tuck in tight to Jesus, our desire will be to live as He intends—according to His Word, His will, and His way.

Are you weary of cultural shifts? Are you weakened by current events? Are you worn out from the voices coming at you from many directions and positions? Then it is time to decide the importance God's Word plays in your life.

The Psalmist made his decision and took his stance. He hated every wrong path because he chose to love God's commands more than gold and considered every one of them to be right. Because he loved God's commands more than gold and considered them to be right, he hated every wrong path. It goes both ways.

Hate is a strong word. When my children were little, we encouraged them to avoid the word. Instead, we taught them that they needed to use *dislike*. "I dislike tomatoes," sounds better coming from a little one than, "I hate tomatoes!"

Because *wrong* is on a different plane than tomatoes, hate is an acceptable word. Deceit, false hope, lies, slander, treachery, and vanity are aspects of wrong. Other versions of Psalm 119:128 has *wrong path* as false path, wrong ways, lying ways, and wicked ways.

The Message version says, "…I despise every deceitful detour" (Psalm 119:128). How do we avoid spiritual detours? We love God's commands more than gold and consider His precepts to be right, meaning ethically straightforward and upright.

When we misstep, falter, or take a wrong turn on our faith journey, we need God's commands to straighten us up and set us right once again. Because He loves us He has commands for us to avoid wrong paths and to live right.

KEY POINT TO DAILY STAND: Knowing God's commands is not enough; we must also love them more than gold and consider them right.

Day 24

Open

KEY VERSE: *I open my mouth and pant, longing for your commands. Psalm 119:131*

It is impossible for a dog to pant with a closed mouth. Normally, dogs pant when excited, eager, or hot. However, excessive panting may be a sign of a serious issue.

Likewise, with eagerness, followers of Jesus should pant for God's commands every day. But what happens when we face serious issues? A closed soul cannot long and pant for the things of the Lord. We must open our souls and welcome His Word to come in and satisfy our longing.

According to the key verse, notice our responsibility:

- Open mouth
- Pant
- Long

A few years ago it became popular to pick a word for the year. I am not one to follow fads, but for the past few years, before I even asked God if He had one for me, He revealed a word when I least expected it. During Advent of 2021 on a Sunday morning, we were singing "O, Little Town of Bethlehem" when my personal 2022 word jumped out at me. It was as if God shined a spotlight on the word.

Enter.

The lyric says *cast out our sin and enter in, be born in us today*. Entering requires opening. Jesus could not enter the world unless Mary opened her heart to God's will and His way. Jesus cannot enter our lives to cast out the sin until we open our hearts and welcome His presence. God's commands cannot enter a closed soul, and they cannot influence or transform a closed mind.

When we struggle to see God at work, we need to open our minds to His Word. As we face hardship and trouble, we must open our hearts and pant for His commands. When we suffer loss, pain, or unmet expectations, it is good to long for God's promises.

When we spiritually drown, we must invite Jesus to bring us above the waters of weariness and worry and open our hearts, gasping and panting and breathing in the Word of God. But if we do not know the Word of God, how can it influence or inspire us to live as Jesus intends?

KEY POINT TO DAILY STAND: Opened Bibles will not open souls. Opened souls need opened Bibles.

Day 25

Distress or Delight?

KEY VERSE: *Trouble and distress have come upon me, but your commands are my delight. Psalm 119:143*

Why is it that some expect being a Christian means easy living, when God promises persecution and trouble? The answers vary, but sometimes in our search for the answers to such questions, we end up avoiding the solutions God already established in His Word.

Giving thanks in all circumstances (1 Thessalonians 5:18), considering trials pure joy (James 1:2), and praising God through suffering (1 Peter 4:16) are not directions to focus on the hardship; rather, they are directives that steer us from distress and point us to delight.

Mrs. Lettie Cowman wrote my favorite devotional book, *Streams in the Desert*. On March 3, she says:

> *When we are born again,*
> *it is not into a soft and protected nursery*
> *but into the open countryside,*
> *where we actually draw our strength from the*
> *distress of the storm.*

Strength from distress? Absolutely! We will never grow deep spiritual roots if we only seek delight through easy living. Delight is not found in our circumstances; it is rooted in us through God's commands, as we walk by faith, and stand firm on Christ, the Solid Rock!

The Psalmist was candid, "Trouble and distress have come upon me…" (Psalm 119:143), but two verses before he said, "…I am lonely and despised…" (Psalm 119:141).

Lonely. Despised. Trouble. Distress. Hardships are internal and external, but God is eternal and internally places

His promises in those who observe His commands. Amid the trials of life, no matter the difficulty, our perspective and *go-to* for delight, should be the same as the Psalmist:

- God's laws are right (Psalm 119:137).
- His statutes are trustworthy (Psalm 119:138).
- His law is true (Psalm 119:142).
- God's statutes are forever right (Psalm 119:144).

Before Kevin and I married, we claimed Psalm 37:4 as a theme verse. *Delight yourself in the Lord and He will give you the desires of your heart.* It is found on mugs, tee shirts, and wall art. But before it makes us feel good, we must contextually apply it to our lives. Taking exquisite delight is *in* the Lord, not the desires *of* our heart.

Many things precede God giving us our desires:

- Do not fret or be envious (Psalm 37:1).
- Trust in the Lord (Psalm 37:3).
- Do good (Psalm 37:3).
- Dwell in the land and enjoy safe pasture (Psalm 37:3).

We serve a God of order. If we only dwell and enjoy, we miss the intended order. God is sovereign and providential—what He deems as *safe pasture* we may see as trouble and distress.

What if God intends to use a distressing situation to draw you closer to Him or to witness to another? Will you allow distress to oppress your mind, or will you delight in His commands to settle your soul?

KEY POINT TO DAILY STAND: "He will surely give you rest by trusting in His Word" (John H. Stockton, 1874, *Only Trust Him*).

Day 26

Nearness

KEY VERSE: *Yet, you are near, O Lord, and all your commands are true. Psalm 119:151*

What would happen if we used God's commands as a starting point every day instead of figuring out how to apply them when hardship happens? This verse declares two things:

- God is near.
- His commands are true.

First, remember, the little words make a big difference. How many commands are true? All of them! And because they are true, they are also trustworthy.

Next, it would appear there are no conditions connected to the declarations. However, Psalm 145:18 says the nearness of God *is* conditional. "The Lord is near to all who call on him, to all who call on him in truth."

Calling on the Lord looks different for each of us and may depend on the situation. The original word means to call out loudly or to cry for help. Our cries and calls for help should be directed to the ear of God. But calling on Him cannot neglect or ignore His commands. They are linked and connected; interwoven and inseparable.

Perhaps when we feel distant from God it is because we left out the *in truth* part. Seeking God must be done on His terms—in truth. Many things lead us astray; therefore, we need His truth.

This past Sunday at my church a few lyrics to "The Battle Hymn of the Republic" were sung by the choir. I was struck as they sang *His truth is marching on*. In Christian culture today many believe *truth marches on*, but that is not true! *His* truth is what marches on; *His* truth leads and guides; *His* truth is necessary for us to use as we call on and cry out to the Lord. And *His* truth is mandatory to experience the nearness of God.

If we rely on *our* truth or *their* truth or any truth other than *His* truth, then we will be distant and distracted, not near to the One we claim to follow.

We can only draw near to the Lord if we claim His truth. And we can claim His truth because we are near to the Lord. Inseparable?

Indeed!

KEY POINT TO DAILY STAND: God cannot be separated from His truth!

Day 27

Faithless

KEY VERSE: *I look on the faithless with loathing, for they do not obey your word. Psalm 119:158*

In the traditional marriage vows, the man and the woman each pledge to *keep to* the other. *Obey* was once commonly used, but through cultural influence in most settings, it has been replaced. As we know, culture gets things wrong. The English word obey implies an authority is involved. However, if we used *obey* in the same manner as today's key verse, it would be an applicable word to insert back into the wedding vows.

The original word for obey used in the key verse means to preserve, watch over, and keep. If I pledged to obey Kevin until death parts us, it means I made a promise to watch over our marriage, to preserve my vows, and to keep faithful to my husband.

However, for those who stood at an altar or made vows knowingly in the sight of God, we pledged nothing to the one we married. Our promise was to God, the one who created covenant and ordained oneness. Covenant requires faithfulness. Therefore, obedience is not to our spouse, but rather to our Lord, who is our authority.

In our relationship with God, it is essential we preserve, watch over, and keep His promises. We are to obey the commands we are called to observe. When we stop observing them, we cease preserving them.

One cannot become faithless unless they were first faithful. We are born faithless. We cannot be faithful to God until we enter into a relationship with Him through Jesus.

There is no question how the Psalmist felt about those who once served and loved God but chose to stop observing His commands and walked away from His ways.

To be clear, the Psalmist did not loath anyone, he simply saw them for what they were—faithless. Other versions say transgressors, treacherous, disloyal, traitors, lawbreakers, and quitters.

Noticing those who are faithless is not standing in judgment over them. Too many Christians buy into the lie that when we notice other believers choosing to live in sin, it is no one else's business to judge them. Well, they are wrong! If found faithless it takes a faithful follower to point out our loathsome behavior. That is love, not judgment!

Preserving, watching over, and keeping God's commands protects the covenant we have with the Lord. As we observe God's commands, we are faithful to the covenant. It is a privilege to preserve God's commands and an honor to watch over His precepts. And we know true joy and experience a peace that passes all understanding as we are faithful to keep and obey God's commands.

KEY POINT TO DAILY STAND: Faith minus God's commands equals faithless.

Day 28

Have an Eye for the I's

KEY VERSION: *I wait for your salvation, O Lord, and I follow your commands. I obey your statutes, for I love them greatly. I obey your precepts and your statutes, for all my ways are known to you. Psalm 119:166-168*

Years ago, I was encouraged to write a manifesto. It is a declaration describing my intentions and motivations.
It begins with:

*SLOW is my mantra: **S**erve God, **L**ove God, **O**bserve His commands, **W**alk in all His ways.*

SLOW shows up often in my teaching, writing, and speaking. But before others can be influenced by it, I strive to live by it. I use my manifesto as a form of personal accountability. If I say it, I better live it. If I declare it, then it ought to be a truism—evident and obvious.

It ends with what I am committed and called to:

Following Jesus: my joy
Devoted to Kevin: my vow
Mom to six: my honor and privilege
Studying and teaching God's Word: my delight
Speaking: my call
Writing: my challenge

And in the middle are declarations of how I choose to live:

Whole, not holes, for my soul.
Doing the right thing matters a lot.
Intuition guides; discernment protects.

Thrive, rather than survive.
Jesus alone determines my identity.
No manipulation, gossip, pettiness, bitterness,
or chaos allowed.
Falling to pieces in a crisis is not an option.
Bold and brave. Fighter and fearless. Virtue and valor.
Laughing out loud. Deep conversations. Spontaneity.
Truth above all.

It is imperative that we have eyes for all that we declare. The words of any manifesto are only ink blots on paper or fonts on a screen. They do not become a truism until they are lived out.

In Psalm 119:166-168, the Psalmist had eyes for some I's:

- I wait for your salvation.
- I follow your commands.
- I obey your statutes.
- I love [your commands] greatly.
- I obey your precepts.

The Psalmist had eyes for the I's because he was aware of Who had eyes on him! "…for all my ways are known to you" (Psalm 119:168b).

How would we live differently if we acknowledged that God first has His eyes on us before we declare or denounce a mantra or manifesto? The Psalmist makes it clear—God is watching us. Too many people think He hovers over us to catch us doing wrong, when really, He watches over us to guide us to live right!

KEY POINT TO DAILY STAND: God loves us too much to take His eyes off us. Therefore, we should have eyes for the I's.

Day 29

A Tuned Heart

KEY VERSE: *May my tongue sing of our word, for all your commands are righteous. Psalm 119:172*

My son Jaylen is an accomplished pianist. No one knew he could play the piano until a year after we adopted him. When he was in second grade, we came home from church one Sunday and we heard him playing a song from worship that morning on a toy keyboard. Months later, he began piano lessons which quickly led to classical training.

One day our microwave and oven timers simultaneously went off. Jaylen's hands went to his ears, and he shouted, "That is not a good sound!" Musically, the two beeps clashed, and my pitch-perfect son was immediately annoyed. Another time we were backing out of a parking spot in the golf cart at our summer place. As the back-up sound warned others of our maneuver, Jaylen said, "Hey, Momma! Did you know that is an F# our golf cart plays?"

He was completely unaware of his ability to know the exact pitch of any sound; it just came naturally—but it did not get exposed until his ability was revealed.

Our hearts will not be in tune with God's Word until we are attuned to God's commands. Knowing His Word and living our way is like the two clashing sounds in Jaylen's ears: unmelodious and inharmonious.

In 1758, Robert Robison wrote the lyrics to the hymn "Come, Thou Fount of Every Blessing." The second line says, *tune my heart to sing thy grace.* Appreciate the order here. God tunes, we sing. We sing because we have something to sing about. At one time after penning the hymn, Mr. Robison was out of tune, because his life was out of order. Years later, he was seated in a stagecoach alongside a woman who started humming the tune to his hymn.

God used the very song He gave to Robert to turn the wandering man back to the Lord. Mr. Robison's heart was tuned again to *sing thy grace*. And with those *streams of mercy never ceasing*, he was called to sing *songs of loudest praise*.

God's Word gives us much to sing about! His commands are righteous and lead us to live in harmony with our Savior if we remain attuned to Him.

KEY QUESTION TO DAILY STAND: What tune will be on your tongue today?

Day 30

Be Sheep

KEY VERSE: *I have strayed like a lost sheep. Seek your servant, for I have not forgotten your commands.* **Psalm 119:176**

Forty-seven years ago, every day for weeks, my seventh-grade math teacher, Mr. Evans, repeated, "There are four quarts in a gallon." His repetitive words continue to ring in my head every time I need to measure something in quarts.

We use fractions when baking and for reading musical scores. A basic understanding of history helps us appreciate our national freedoms. Hints like *i before e except after c* and the little ditty *conjunction junction, what's your function* help us not forget important grammar guidelines. There are many things we learned as a student that we will never forget.

Likewise, when it comes to God's commands, though we cannot memorize them all, we will become familiar with them as we spend time in His Word.

In today's key verse the Psalmist confesses to straying but admits he did not forget God's commands. Like an effective teacher who uses repetition to cement a lesson, the Psalmist relies on the commands God had taught.

We are no different from the Psalmist; we too, stray. But that is not an excuse for us to forget God's Word and neglect His ways. His commands keep us on track, but they also get us back on the right path when we veer off course. Jesus will never lead us astray, but like sheep, we can easily stray from the pastures provided by God and the safety of our Good Shepherd (John 10:11,14).

Sheep are lost without their shepherd. The sheep are not called to find safe pasture or grassy fields. Lost sheep cannot find their way back. They need their shepherd. Some need search and rescue; others need to be sought and brought back. They are incapable of fighting off predators and avoiding harmful terrain. That is the role of a shepherd.

Sheep learn the voice of the shepherd. And when they know his voice, they can heed his commands and closely follow. That is why we, as sheep, need to observe God's commands—so we can remain tucked in tight to Jesus, our Good Shepherd.

But we can only observe what we do not forget. Therefore, we must be SLOW-livin' sheep: Serving God, Loving God, Observing His commands, and Walking in all His ways.

KEY POINT TO DAILY STAND: Be a sheep who trusts the Shepherd.

When we walk with the Lord
in the light of His Word
What a glory He sheds on our way!
While we do His good will,
He abides with us still
And with all who will trust and obey

Trust and obey,
for there's no other way
To be happy in Jesus,
but to trust and obey.

"Trust and Obey"
John H. Sammis

BOOK 4
STAND daily
Walking in all God's Ways

"And now, O Israel, what does the Lord require of you but to fear the Lord...to walk in all God's ways..."
Deuteronomy 10:12-13

Throughout the next thirty days, each daily reading will come from the eleventh chapter of Hebrews.

Each day's reading is set up in the same manner:

- Title
- Key Verse
- Key Content
- Key Point

These daily readings are designed to encourage you to grow, challenge you to change, and influence you to live as Jesus intends:

SLOW

Day 1

Never Ending Witness

KEY VERSE: *By faith Abel still speaks…Hebrews 11:4*

Hebrews 11 is commonly known as the Hall of Faith. The first person mentioned is not the first man to walk Earth. Rather, it is his son Abel. Legacy and heritage are important, but they are not required to walk in all God's ways. A personal relationship with God is the first step to walking by faith.

Adam and Eve raised their children in the same place we all come from: outside the Garden of Eden. And just like each of us, their children had to choose the path they would take in life—to walk by faith or to walk by sight; to regulate our life by God's standards or to set our own.

Today's key verse hints at how one of Adam's sons lived. But it also comparatively tells of another. Abel walked by faith and was commended as righteous. But when sin crouched at Cain's door, instead of walking over or around it, he welcomed it in and regulated his life to it (Genesis 4:7).

Both brothers left a legacy. After Cain killed Abel, he became a restless wanderer and walked away from the Lord's presence (Genesis 4:14-16). However, though Abel was dead, according to Hebrews 11:4, his walk of faith still lives on. "By faith [Abel] still speaks, even though he is dead."

Cain and Abel both offered sacrifices to the Lord. Genesis 4:3 says Cain brought some of the fruit, but Genesis 4:4 reports Abel brought fat portions from his flock. Cain brought *some* while Abel offered *the best*. Abel's sacrifice was acceptable because he gave with his heart and was careful, selective, and sacrificial in his offering. Cain was careless and thoughtless. Some might think the gift is enough, but walking by faith is a matter of the heart;

therefore, motivation and intent matter.

Many churches have plaques inscribed with the names of persons who gave certain gifts, or there are walls of inscriptions of those who monetarily made a building grow. Names on insignias prove a gift was given, but they do not commend a walk of faith. Only God knows the motivation and intent of a heart. Bigger buildings do not leave legacies of faith. Faithful followers who regulate their life according to God's ways are commended for their faith—especially after they die.

How Able gave and *why* he sacrificed left a legacy of faith—not *what* he gave and *where* it was used. His faith journey is a never-ending witness of faithfully walking in all God's ways.

Walking in all God's ways walks by faith every day and then every day after we are gone, others can still be influenced by our faith journey.

KEY POINT TO DAILY STAND: *By faith* cannot get by on second best or a careless walk of faith.

Day 2

Taken

KEY VERSE: *By faith Enoch was taken...Hebrews 11:5*

There are two persons in all of history to have never experienced an earthly death. Both are in the Bible: Elijah and Enoch. Today's key verse records, "...[Enoch] could not be found, because God had taken him away." In Hebrews 11:5 the word *taken* in the New International Version is used three times:

- Enoch was *taken* from this life (Hebrews 11:5a).
- God had *taken* Enoch away (Hebrews 11:5b).
- Before Enoch was *taken*, he was commended (Hebrews 11:5c).

First, the original word means to transport or change or remove. In a blink Enoch's body and soul were gone from Earth and transported to glory! He was never pronounced dead; he was just declared *no more*. "...because God took him away" (Genesis 5:24).

Next, anyone adopted into the family of God enters by way of Jesus (John 1:12). And like Enoch, though their bodies return to the dust of the ground, God takes those souls away and, in a blink, they are transported to their eternal home with Jesus.

How Enoch lived—walking in all God's ways—is how he got mentioned in the Hall of faith, not how he died. Though he was taken from earth before his body died, Enoch lived to please God.

Finally, it is imperative to note Enoch's commendation because it should also be said of us. *If* we walk in all God's ways, it *will* be said of us. "...was commended as one who pleased God" (Hebrews 11:5c).

To gratify God entirely, we must walk by faith. To wholly walk by faith, we must walk in all God's ways. God is pleased with those who walk His way. Genesis 5:24 simply states, "Enoch walked with God," and years later the Holy Spirit inspired the writer of Hebrews to commend the man and name him in the Hall of Faith.

The original word for *walk* in Genesis 5:24 is also the *W* in SLOW livin'. Walking in all God's ways will not get us taken to glory without a physical death, but it will allow us to not get overtaken by sin as we continue to live on Earth.

We are all taken by something—our finances, reputation, habits, relationships, tragedies, and more! To faithfully walk in all God's ways, we must take everything that threatens to carry us away and place it under the Lordship of Jesus Christ.

KEY THOUGHT TO DAILY STAND: If you have gotten carried away by anything other than Jesus, ask Him to take away whatever stands in the way of truly walking by faith.

Day 3

Holy Fear

KEY VERSE: ***By faith Noah…in holy fear built an ark to save his family.* Hebrews 11:7**

Noah built an Ark because God told him to do it. The corruption on earth was very bad—evil was prevalent and out of control—so God made His judgment: everything in the Ark would be safe; everything outside of it would suffer and perish. Everyone outside of Noah's family thought he was a crazy person when he started building a floating vessel.

But Noah did not care what the people thought—he was not afraid of them; rather, he had a holy fear of what would happen should he not walk by faith. Genesis 6:9 says, "Noah was a righteous man, blameless among the people of his time, and he walked with God." And hundreds of years later, Noah's story continues to get taught and his walk of faith commended.

Noah walked in all God's ways. Genesis 6 ends with, "Noah did everything just as God commanded him." *Everything* and *all* are simple words with a massive impact. If Noah refused to do what God had commanded, he could not be commended for walking in all God's ways. Blameless is not sinless; it is faultless. Noah was found to not be at fault regarding the corruption that everyone else was participating in during the time he built the Ark.

Holy fear keeps us living in holiness. A holy fear is more afraid of what will happen should we disobey the Lord than how others react and respond to our faith stance.

A holy fear will never have us frozen in fear. Yet, Christians today are fearful of what is going on around them. And this anxiety has them stuck on their faith journey. A holy fear propels us to stand firm; a holy fear prepares us to fight the good fight of faith; a holy fear pushes us to do what is right!

Our faith stance is not solely for us; we have friends and family who need to be saved from whatever has a hold on them. Followers of Jesus have the answer! But if we do not live like we know the answer, how can those around us be saved?

Jesus is our Ark of Safety—anyone found in Him is freed and safe. Oh, the world around us continues to be crazy and chaotic, but when we are in the Ark we can boldly and blindly walk by faith amid the mayhem.

It is time followers of Jesus live like we are aboard the Ark and stop hiding below deck where our faith journey cannot be seen! It is time we stop giving more airtime and facetime to the things we are afraid of and stand firm on the foundation of our faith! Jesus Christ!

KEY POINT TO DAILY STAND: Walking by faith needs a holy fear to keep us from being frozen in fear.

Day 4

Even Though

KEY VERSE: *By faith Abraham…obeyed and went…even though…Hebrews 11:8*

When an *even though* is inserted into a thought, it emphasizes the truth of a preceding fact. In Hebrews 11:8 we read Abraham obeyed God and went where God told him to go *even though* he did not know where he was going. That is the very definition of a walk of faith: obediently doing what God says and going where He sends.

Knowing the details of the specific duties and plans God has for each of us will not have us walking by faith. The *even though* regarding Abraham speaks volumes about his faith journey. It is easy to walk where we see the terrain and can plan for our next steps, but it requires reliance on God, trust in His Word, and strength only found in Jesus to walk by faith.

The call of Abraham is found in Genesis 12:1, "The Lord said…leave and go…" But his walk of faith began in Genesis 12:4. "So Abram left." (Before God changed his name, it was Abram.) He was seventy-five years old.

My friend Bill was about eighty years old when I met him. Bill loved Jesus with his whole heart! But he did not always walk by faith. He told me his salvation story. When he and his wife were in their mid-forties, Ruth was invited to a special weekly worship service called a revival—an opportunity for Christians to have their faith reawakened and for unsaved folks to get saved.

Bill was not excited to go, and while the guest evangelist preached, Bill fell asleep. He said, "As I woke up I thought Ruth started walking out. I figured it was time to leave, but instead I followed her to the altar and did what she did: I repented of my sin and invited Jesus into my life! I figured if it was good enough for Ruth, it was good enough for me."

Even though Bill did not hear one word from the Bible, nor paid any attention to the preaching, the man was saved! And from that day forward until God called them home, Bill and Ruth walked in all God's ways and lived for Jesus every day!

KEY POINT TO DAILY STAND: Walking by faith walks all the way, every day, *even though* many things hinder the way.

Day 5

Live Like a Stranger

KEY VERSE: *By faith Abraham made his home...like a stranger...Hebrews 11:9*

Months after our two youngest children were adopted, my husband was appointed to a different church. Jaylen and Sukanya were barely acclimated to their new home when our address changed. This abrupt transfer necessitated that Kevin and I teach our impressionable children what *home* meant.

As a pastor's family in an itinerant denomination, we do not pick and choose where we live. Kevin is under the authority of leadership who make that decision. Therefore, we needed to introduce and instill what our older four kids already accepted and acclimated to: the house we live in is the structure we dwell in, but wherever our family lands is where we call home.

Abraham made his home where God told him to go, but until the occupants left, he lived like a stranger amongst them. The people of God, the Israelites, did not inhabit the Promised Land until hundreds of years later.

Home is where our citizenship lies. As children of God, we know heaven is our home. According to Peter's first letter, he urges Christians to live as aliens and strangers in the world (1 Peter 2:11). Perhaps you have heard the statement *be in the world, not of it*.

Many wonder how we can live like strangers in a broken world amongst people who are spiritually lost. How will they know Jesus if we are living as strangers? The charge does not mean we keep non-Christians at an arm's length; rather, living like strangers avoids and rejects worldly ways but still engages and embraces people.

Walking in all God's ways, keeps us aligned with His

will, not adhering to the ways of the world. Many things, like chaos and confusion, are not part of God's home; they belong to the world and precede corruption. Though we dwell in a land filled with chaos, amongst people who are confused—by embracing and approving all sorts of corruption, we are called and expected to live as aliens—those who do not belong.

Living like a stranger is protection for us by an omniscient God and loving Father. When we live in the world surrounded by ungodly influences like we belong there, we step outside of His protective bounds and no longer walk in all His ways. Therefore, God charges us to live as strangers so that we do not become comfortable or tempted to partake or participate in the chaos and confusion that abounds all around.

KEY POINT TO DAILY STAND: Living like a stranger seems strange, but we are charged to do it.

Day 6

Foundations

KEY VERSE: *By faith Abraham looked forward to the city with foundations...Hebrews 11:10*

Foundation matters.

Shortly after Kevin and I started dating, I moved to Miami, Florida, for a year, while Kevin remained in Michigan. A couple of years after we married in the spring of 1993, Kevin and I went to a friend's wedding in Miami. It was just months after Hurricane Andrew wreaked havoc in the southern state.

While there friends took us on a tour, but I found I hardly recognized the place. Some landmarks were simply piles of rubble. Most notably was a subdivision where some other friends used to live. Though their house stood tall and appeared sturdy, it was condemned. Like many structures, it fell prey to the damaging winds as it was shifted a couple of inches off its foundation.

Foundation matters.

It did not take long after we adopted our two youngest to realize a large part of adopting children who are older requires recognizing our parenting and love was not the primary foundation in their lives. After only a few years with one biological parent, who later had their parental rights terminated, plus a temporary, but lengthy, stay in a foster home—even though there were unhealthy cracks and harmful crevices—foundations were still laid.

It was never our responsibility to undo what was done, but because foundations matter God entrusted us to lay what He deemed right and best. And just like all six of our children, it was never our duty to make any of them walk by faith. It was only our assignment to introduce and lead our kids to the Architect and Builder of the only foundation that matters!

By faith Abraham looked forward to the same city we all are destined to dwell in, but we can only enter this city if we stand on and trust in the only true foundation that matters. The writer of the letter to the Hebrews said, "For Abraham was looking forward to the city with foundations, whose architect and builder is God" (Hebrews 11:10).

Today's key verse connects two *by faith* assertions regarding Abraham:

- By faith he lived like a stranger (see Day 5).
- By faith he was enabled to be a father (see Day 7).

Knowing and trusting the Architect and Builder of the foundation we rely on matter to our faith journey. We can only live by faith and walk in all God's ways if we stand firm on the foundation that matters: Jesus Christ, the Solid Rock.

KEY POINT TO DAILY STAND: Any ground other than Jesus is sinking sand!

Day 7

Enabled

KEY VERSE: *By faith Abraham, even though he was past age—and Sarah herself was barren—was enabled to become a father...Hebrews 11:11*

Enablement is not entitlement! When God called Abraham to follow Him, his wife Sarah was sixty-five and he was seventy-five, and they were promised a child. But we can see from the key verse that she was unable to get pregnant, and they were well past their childbearing years.

However, for a follower of Jesus, the beautiful thing about spiritual enablement is that it has nothing to do with what we are capable of and has everything to do with God enabling something outside the scope of probability and within the limitless possibilities of an Almighty God.

It is astounding how Abraham and Sarah walked by faith *after* hearing Abraham would be made into a great nation. Inheritance requires an heir and they had no one in their bloodline to make good on that promise. But the Promise-keeper does not make promises He never intends to keep!

Walking by faith will not see the promises of God on our timetable. Walking in all His ways trusts His promises will come and enables us to wait and wander well. Abraham and Sarah waited twenty-five years for their promised son.

Entitlement is self-seeking; therefore, enablement acknowledges and trusts Jesus. God did for Abraham what the man could not do for himself; God gave Abraham what He promised, not what Abraham sought; God enabled Abraham's seed to come to life in his wife's barren womb!

When we see someone as a lost cause and too far gone for God to move, perhaps we need to pray for the divine enablement to open their closed and dried-up soul and watch new life spring up in what appears to be a barren wasteland. After all, God never wastes a wasteland, and He can enable and enact His Spirit to inject hope into any hopeless situation.

KEY CONSIDERATION TO DAILY STAND: Consider what hopeless situation is present in your life. By faith, pray, "Our God is able to enable _____."

Day 8

Reasoning

KEY VERSE: ***By faith Abraham, reasoned that God could raise the dead…Hebrews 11:19***

The original word for *reasoned* in today's key verse means to come to the bottom line or take into account or to come to a logical conclusion.

Reasoning cannot come *before* we walk by faith; otherwise, we would most likely stop walking our faith journey. Abraham reasoned that God could raise the dead *after* he passed the ultimate test from God.

Hebrews 11:17 says, "By faith Abraham, when God tested him, offered Isaac as a sacrifice…" Isaac was Abraham's promised son. Some believe it stands to reason that a loving God would never ask Abraham to sacrifice his son. Therefore, in matters of faith, we need to set reason aside. Before we focus on the son, we need to see a man who wholeheartedly walked by faith and who took God at His word.

Too many Christians are too busy reasoning with God; thereby, missing a mark of a disciple: to walk by faith. SLOW livin' followers walk in all God's ways, all the way our Savoir leads—even when it does not make sense.

Yesterday, my husband preached at the Chapel service of our summer place. His theme? *When God Doesn't Make Sense.* As the people entered, we received two copper pennies. As he preached, the play on words was not lost as Kevin challenged us to consider the *change* God makes in our lives and to pay attention when God does not make *sense*.

Jesus will not have our attention if we are trying to get to the bottom line on what God is up to or if we frustratingly search for a logical conclusion of what He is asking of us. Before we reason, we need a moment of reckoning, a spiritual timeout, to step back and allow God to deal with our lack of faith and settle our souls so we can live *by faith,* listed alongside Abraham in the Hall of Faith.

When God asked Abraham to sacrifice Isaac, there was much more going on behind the scenes—out of sight from any reasoning or logical explanation. Imagine the lessons young Isaac learned as he witnessed his daddy faithfully follow God, trusting His provision through every unknown step they took up Mt. Moriah to the altar where sacrifices were made.

As they ascended, Isaac inquired about the sacrifice asking, "Where is the lamb?" (Genesis 22:7). And Abraham responded, "God himself will provide…" (Genesis 22:8).

Abraham kept walking by faith, never reasoning out the moment or questioning the Lord. He never gave up on God—even when he bound Isaac, laid him on the altar, and raised his knife above his son—even then, Abraham walked by faith.

Abraham was willing to follow the Lord all the way, never reasoning out what might happen; rather, choosing to walk in all God's ways.

KEY SONG TO DAILY STAND: "All the Way My Savior Leads Me," Fanny Crosby, 1875

All the way my Savior leads me–What have I to ask beside?
  Can I doubt His tender mercy,
  Who through life has been my guide?
  Heav'nly peace, divinest comfort,
  Here by faith in Him to dwell!
For I know, whate'er befall me, Jesus doeth all things well;
For I know, whate'er befall me, Jesus doeth all things well.

Day 9

Still Living When Dead

KEY VERSE: *All these people were still living by faith when they died. Hebrews 11:13*

On July 22, 2018, my mom died. That same day, at the exact moment she took her last breath, she was still living. It is paradoxical to die, and yet, live. But that is the way of the kingdom! Every time her husband, three daughters, and their families talk of her walk with the Lord, her faith lives on. Mom was not overly overt in her faith journey, but by faith, she lived steady and true to her Lord, and that still lives on!

Hebrews 11:12 reports, "From [Abraham]…came descendants as numerous as the stars in the sky and as countless as the sand on the seashore." The key verse refers to the numerous and countless folks as *these people*. The writer of Hebrews says *they* lived like strangers in the land, and though *they* did not receive the things promised, *these people* forged forward, looking to the promises from a distance and never looking back on what they left (Hebrews 11:13-15).

Kevin and I are nearing the age of retirement. It is a weird thing for us. Not because we do not want to grow old; rather, though Kevin will one day retire as a full-time pastor, we will never tire of walking by faith and going where God sends and doing what God says!

Too many people our age, and older, make plans and live their lives so they can leave their kids their money and belongings.

In the planning, they leave out the most important legacy of all: a life lived by faith. There is nothing wrong with leaving an inheritance, but if it stands taller than our faith, it will be a waste.

The thought of my descendants enjoying our belongings versus them seeing us still living by faith after we die is a no-brainer—Kevin and I choose to walk in all God's ways today so that when we die, we will still be living by faith when we are walking those streets of gold!

KEY QUESTION TO DAILY STAND: We all have a choice: will we live by faith now so we can still live by faith after we die?

Day 10

Blessing

KEY VERSE: *By faith Isaac blessed Jacob and Esau in regard to their future. Hebrews 11:20*

During a funeral or memorial, it is common to hear a eulogy. The word comes from the Greek word, *eulogeó*. It means to speak well of.

When my grandpa turned eighty, my mom and her siblings gave him a party. My husband had the idea to give everyone an opportunity to speak well of grandpa. Yes, we gave him his eulogy ten years before he died! It was perfectly beautiful to look over at him as he received blessing after blessing from his family and friends.

The fathers of our faith begin in order: Abraham, Isaac, and Jacob. Though Abraham had one son, Isaac had twins. Only one is named in the lineage that matters most to our faith journey, the genealogy of Jesus (Matthew 1:2). However, in today's key verse, the writer of Hebrews names both brothers.

Parents ought to speak well of their kids—even if they do not seemingly deserve it! The Isaac Family was not always harmonious. At times, sin reigned. Favoritism, deception, jealousy, and manipulation. But a perfect family is not the point. People who repent, take responsibility, right a wrong, apologize, and forgive are some keys to a family who live by faith!

Even amid the family dysfunction, Isaac blessed his sons. And God saw fit to use this bloodline as the conduit to bring Jesus Christ into the world! And He even allowed them to be named in the Hall of Faith—not for their indiscretions; rather, for God's amazing grace to be on display!

For thirty-three years now my husband has done a beautiful job of blessing our six kids. Oh, they would not tell you their daddy has eulogized them, but neither can they tell you he has missed the mark or neglected to speak well of them. When it comes to parenting, Kevin and I desire to live a *no-regret* and *by-faith* life toward our children and grandchildren.

Blessing them in adulthood involves, but is not limited to:

- cheering them on from the sidelines
- championing them
- listening
- being present from a distance
- encouraging their faith journey
- sharing wisdom
- apologizing
- deep and meaningful conversation
- respecting their oneness in marriage
- genuinely complimenting commendable matters

Blessing also involves things we will never do:

- create guilt trips
- manipulate
- compete with in-laws
- parent their children
- turn a blind eye to sinful choices
- offer opinion without being asked
- engage in idle chit-chat
- gossip about them

Isaac blessed his boys *in regard to their future*. Speaking well of someone positions them to face the future. Pointing them to the One who holds their future is paramount and influences their faith journey.

KEY POINT TO DAILY STAND: We cannot speak well of someone if we have our eyes on self.

I am weak but Thou art strong;
Jesus, keep me from all wrong;
I'll be satisfied as long
As I walk, let me walk close to Thee.

Just a closer walk with Thee,
Grant it, Jesus, is my plea,
Daily walking close to Thee,
Let it be, dear Lord, let it be.

"Just a Closer Walk with Thee"
Anonymous

Day 11

Leaning

KEY VERSE: *By faith Jacob, when he was dying, blessed each of his sons, and worshiped as he leaned on the top of his staff. Hebrews 11:21*

Notice the verbs in today's key verse:

- Blessed
- Worshiped
- Leaned

On Day 10 the focus was blessing. Just like his father did when he *blessed* him and his brother, Jacob followed suit with his twelve sons. But there are two more actions attributed to how Jacob lived by faith.

Worship. The original word means to do reverence; to fall down on a knee in worship; to obeisance. Perhaps this is a new word for you, too. It is a movement of the body to express a deep respect or deferential courtesy.

Leaned. In English we need the two words to explain the one Greek word. Worship is deferential. Deference is a respectful submission and yielding to another. Every time we worship the Lord it should involve leaning.

We cannot wholly lean on Jesus' name and simultaneously stand on sinking sand. We cannot listen to God's wisdom while leaning on our own wiles. We cannot fix our eyes on Jesus when our ears are bent to cultural whims.

Jacob leaned on his staff. The imagery is that in his weakened state, Jacob could not stand on his own; therefore, he used the staff to lean on as if it were total dependence on the One who held him. The blessing involved words, the leaning implied worship. Though the old man was weak, he would not neglect worship nor praise to the Lord.

Jacob, and all the others named in the Hall of Faith, truly desired to finish well. How we end has significant meaning and spiritual influence on our loved ones. We can tell them about our wishes for them, but we must show them how to live by faith to the very end.

In 1894 through his well-known hymn "Leaning on the Everlasting Arms," Mr. E. A. Hoffman named spiritual advantages and benefits to leaning on the everlasting arms of Jesus!

A fellowship and a joy divine
A blessedness and peace that is mine
Being safe and secure from all alarms
Noting how sweet it is to walk in this pilgrim way
How bright the path grows from day to day
We have nothing to dread
We have nothing to fear
We gain a blessed peace because our Lord is so near

KEY POINT TO DAILY STAND: Walking in all God's ways, trusting in His Word, and relying on the everlasting arms of Jesus have holy dividends we can never acquire through earthly means.

Day 12
Speak About

KEY VERSE: *By faith Joseph, when his end was near, spoke about... Hebrews 11:22*

How we live certainly matters, but how we end, matters, too! When his end was near, notice what Joseph *did not* talk about:

- how his brothers were jealous of him
- how his brothers planned to murder him
- how his brothers opted to sell him into slavery
- how his brothers lied to their father about his supposed death
- when he was promoted as a high-ranking official
- when he was falsely accused of rape
- when he spent time in prison
- when he strategized to save Egypt from a famine
- when he directed a family reunion with his brothers
- when he confronted his brothers after years of separation
- when he said, "You intended to harm me, but God intended it for good."
- when he reassured his brothers of his forgiveness and spoke kindly to them

Nope, he did not make mention of any of that near his death. Instead, he chose to speak about the exodus of the Israelites. To avoid starvation Jacob, his wives, all his sons, their wives, and all their children came to Egypt. It was never God's plan for this family to remain in Egypt. He used the famine to reunite a family, not change their address.

The Promised Land was theirs, and they were to head back. Though Egypt became Joseph's home, he knew the importance and significance of being where God willed and not where man orchestrated. Therefore, at the end of his life, it was imperative he live by faith and speak about the exodus from Egypt.

God had promised the land of Canaan to the Jacob Family, not Egypt. Though it was not His hand that sent Joseph there, it was His grace that carried him through all the years he lived in Egypt. But even Joseph knew where home was for his people, the Israelites. They belonged where God said and led—to the land He promised to Abraham.

At the end of life, for those of us who live by faith, we must speak about the things of God: His promises, His love, His grace, His Son, His Word, His will, and His ways.

KEY POINT TO DAILY STAND: There is nothing of greater value, importance, or significance to speak about than Jesus!

Day 13

No Fear

KEY VERSE: *By faith Moses' parents...were not afraid...Hebrews 11:23*

Moses was born during turbulent times. On Day 12 it was mentioned that Joseph spoke about the exodus of the Israelites from Egypt. However, that does not imply his family honored his words. Living by faith is individual, every person will be held accountable according to their personal faith stance. No one gets a pass into glory on the shirttails of their ancestors, and they are not welcomed in based on pedigree.

Joseph spoke about the exodus, but over four hundred years later, at the beginning of the Book of Exodus, we read the Israelites were still there. Though they did not return to the Promised Land, the promises of God were still intact. The Promise Keeper kept His Word, and His people were fruitful and multiplied greatly (Exodus 1:7).

The pharaoh was threatened by their growth and feared the Israelites would join forces with enemy nations and put his kingdom, Egypt, in harm's way. He planned to deal shrewdly with the people, forcing them to work as slaves, making their lives extremely difficult. The plan failed. And the Israelites continued to grow in number.

Then the pharaoh strategized plan B: kill all the baby boys born in the Hebrew (Israelite) camp. He even told the Hebrew midwives his expectations. But they refused to do as the pharaoh ordered, fearing God more than the pharaoh (Exodus 1:17). God even allowed quick and easy deliveries for the pregnant mommas.

Jochebed was one of these women. She was the birth-mom to Moses. God revealed what a fine child Moses was and birthed a plan in his parents to save their son. By faith they hid him; then Jochebed set him afloat on the Nile River. The pharaoh's daughter rescued him and raised God's future deliverer for His people in the palace.

The pharaoh's edict was harsh, and the consequences of disobeying and disregarding his order were fatal. But according to Hebrews 11:23, Moses' parents were not afraid of his edict. Where God was at work, the parents were unaware. He prepared the deliverer before Jochebed delivered Moses, but He instilled in them a deep passion and drive to save their boy.

Providence sees the past, present, and future at once. The parents acted by faith in the moment. As faithful people live by faith, they are compelled by the Spirit of God to participate in His redemptive plans for His good purposes.

Walking in all God's ways lives fearless! It does not require we know the details; we only need to trust the One who gives the orders and calls us to live by faith.

KEY POINT TO DAILY STAND: Fear keeps us from walking in all God's ways; walking by faith lives as Jesus intends—fearless!

Day 14

Hard Choices

KEY VERSE: *By faith Moses...refused to be known as...He chose to be mistreated along with the people of God rather than...Hebrews 11:24-25*

Moses was raised in a palace while his own people, the Israelites, lived in slavery and squalor. For forty years he had the best of everything at his disposal: clothing, food, academia, comforts, jewels. However, the entire time he lived in the palace, he knew where he truly belonged.

After he became a man, he refused to be known as the son of pharaoh's daughter (Hebrews 11:24). Historical records say Moses was an only child and the princess was the pharaoh's only descendant. His royal station came with great expectation. But he refuted and denied the familial and royal connection.

By faith, Moses made the choice to which family he belonged: the people of God. Being pulled in two directions, between differing beliefs and cultural trends, but mostly, balancing spiritual divides was problematic, chaotic, impossible, and went against God's ways.

But that was not the only hard decision he made. Moses was faced with choosing between the pleasures of the palace or being mistreated alongside the people of God. For Moses, being a part of the family of God meant being all-in on all things.

When he aligned with God and began walking by faith, he walked away from the momentary comforts and temporary pleasures from the seasons of sin offered from living in the palace.

The original Greek word for *mistreated*, in Hebrews 11:25, is *sugkakoucheomai*. It is only used this one time. When we consider mistreatment, we tend to think of it as something he individually suffered through. However, we must pay attention to the two words following mistreatment in today's key verse: *along with*. We must combine the phrase *chose to be mistreated along with the people of God* because it defines the one Greek word.

When Moses made this choice, it meant he was willing to share in the people's affliction; to come into their fellowship of adversity; to endure persecution together. He knew exactly what he was signing up for when he chose to be aligned with God's people!

He may not have known the particulars, but Moses did not object to whatever came his way—he walked in all God's ways and willingly took on immense difficulty, stayed alongside his people, and suffered through all that came their way.

KEY QUESTION TO DAILY STAND: How far into hardship are you willing to go to walk by faith alongside your people?

Day 15

Disgrace > Treasure?

KEY VERSE: *By faith Moses regarded disgrace for the sake of Christ as of greater value than the treasures of Egypt...Hebrews 11:26*

If we walked around a cemetery and noticed the inscriptions on grave markers, we would be hard-pressed to find duplicates. *By faith* sets the tone and expectation for the epitaphs in Hebrews 11, and none are fully repeated; they each stand alone.

Epitaph is a noun and a verb, and Hebrews 11 is filled with the brief writings in praise of a deceased person. But the writer also epitaphed many Biblical saints; he commemorated them with praise. And yet, it is so much more!

Moses has the longest commemoration. More is not better or more significant; his is simply longer. But it might be considered more profound, especially regarding today's key verse because the commendation is intense and deep.

Disgrace for the sake of Christ. Other versions use reproach, shame, abuse, scorn, insult, suffering, rebuke, and reproof. What would we think of the individual who had this epitaph inscribed on their gravestone? We can read through the book of Exodus and gain clarity on the life of Moses. But God did not allow it in His Book to only be a history lesson. No! He intends to use it in the lives of all who read it.

Moses knew disgrace. He lived with it; he dealt with it; he suffered through it. But he also allowed God to use it. And when he considered all the treasures of Egypt—those on display and the ones in storehouses—Moses believed there was no comparison between the vast riches and the privilege of suffering for Christ's sake.

Of course, Moses did not know Jesus, but he knew

enough about a God who would protect His covenant and keep His promise of everlasting love. Moses realized there was more going on than what he could see or know. By faith he was *looking ahead to his reward* (Hebrews 11:26b).

The original word for *looking* is only found in Hebrews 11:26. It has two meanings.

1. to turn the eyes away from other things and fix them on some one thing; to look at attentively
2. to look with steadfast mental gaze.

At times we get so caught up in the hard things that we get tunnel vision, or we lose sight of how God just might be at work through our hardship. As followers of Jesus we already know our reward! Since that is so, why do we allow suffering and disgrace to bring us down when we ought to praise the Lord that He can use it for the sake of Christ?

Christians are expected to fix their eyes on Jesus, have a Christ-like mindset, and focus on suffering and disgrace as having far more value to their walk of faith than living on Easy Street.

KEY QUESTION TO DAILY STAND: What has greater value in your life—suffering for the sake of Christ or asking God to remove the hardship?

Day 16

Persevere

KEY VERSE: *By faith Moses left Egypt...[and] persevered because he saw him who is invisible.* **Hebrews 11:27**

Before we look at today's theme, the first four words of today's key verse should not be glossed over.
By faith Moses left.
There are times in our life when God calls us to go and then there are other times, he commands us to leave. For Moses, this was geographical. But for us, it rarely is. And yet, there are things in our life hindering us from walking in all His ways, so God tells us to leave them.

My friends had a dog that would stand in front of them with a ball in its mouth. The furry one desperately wanted to play fetch but would not drop the ball. So my friends would repeat, "Leave it!" Unless the dog released the ball, it would not experience freedom and enjoyment.

Living in ways contrary to God's Word is not walking in all His ways. There are things we must leave. God calls us out, but do we listen? God provides a way out, but do we go? To live right, a *left* is necessary. To wholly cleave to Christ, we must leave what is not holy.

On to the theme: *By faith Moses persevered.*
In the Bible this word for persevere is found only in Hebrews 11:27. It is to endure, be steadfast, and patient. We tend to think of perseverance as something that gets us through difficult or strenuous situations. But if our goal is to *just get through*, then we will surely miss all God has for us as we walk by faith.

Walking in all God's ways willingly perseveres through all the valleys of the shadow of death and into any fiery furnace or lion's den. The goal is not to get through anything, but rather, for God's Word to get through us and for us to walk each step by faith.

Goals are good, but if they are manmade or self-appointed, then we will be hard-pressed to walk by faith, because generally when we set a goal, we also plan it out. Knowing a plan does not involve faith. Having certain plans is prudent, but when God's ways take a backseat, that leaves the driving and navigation to us. And we do not need too many examples of being in the driver's seat of life to know a wreak is imminent.

Moses left and was gone forty years before he came back to deliver God's people out of Egypt. Over those forty years Moses persevered because God revealed the invisible to him. What he could not see bolstered him to endure; what was invisible gave him steadfast strength; he fixed his eyes on what he could not see and patiently persevered.

KEY POINT TO DAILY STAND: Walking by faith may not see what lies ahead; therefore, we must walk in all God's ways to persevere and press on.

Day 17

Sprinkles

KEY VERSE: *By faith [Moses] kept the Passover and the sprinkling of blood, so that the destroyer of the firstborn would not touch the firstborn of Israel. Hebrews 11:28*

    Sprinkles are those multi-colored bits of sugar on a cake or an ice cream cone that bring smiles and happiness to many. How is it that a few tiny, colorful morsels can bring purpose to a lackluster dessert and produce such joy and delight?

    On a hot summer day when I was a child, we spent hours running through the sprinkler. The purpose? It cooled us down, kept us out of the house, brought neighborhood friends together, and caused laughter and amusement among children. How is it sprinkles of water falling on heads can produce such joy and delight?

    In the middle of today's key verse are two words with a major impact: *so that*. Pay attention when these two words are found in Scripture—they denote purpose!

    How is it that the sprinkling of blood can bring such joy and delight? The writer of Hebrews 11:28 tells us. Look at the purpose found after *so that*.

The destroyer of the firstborn would not touch the firstborn of Israel.

    Remember, Israel is known as the Hebrew people, God's chosen people. He made a covenant with them through Abraham. They would be a great nation; He would allow them to be fruitful and multiply and inhabit Canaan, the promised Land.

    In Exodus 12 Moses instituted the Passover, but it was the Lord who commanded it for His people. It was time for their rescue from Egypt. On the night before they walked out of bondage and towards the Promised Land, the death angel would come to any house that did not have the blood of a lamb spread on the sides and top of the doorframes. The instructions from Moses included when and how to prepare the lamb for slaughter and apply the sprinkling of blood to save the firstborn boys from death.

Fast-forward over three thousand years and the blood of the Lamb, sprinkled on the doorframes of our souls, saves us from death and frees us from bondage!

The little words make a big difference. Not *a* lamb; rather, *the* Lamb.

Jesus is *the* Lamb of God. His blood is *the* barrier that covers and forgives sin and makes us right with God *so that* we can be freed from the bondage of sin and the penalty of death and have access to the power over the Devil's destructive ways.

KEY POINT TO DAILY STAND: Walking in all God's ways is the for-sure way to live by faith and to know pure joy and unwavering delight.

Day 18

Passing Through

KEY VERSE: *By faith the people passed through the Red Sea as on dry land...Hebrews 11:29*

Kevin and I love to drive to faraway places. We realize other means are more convenient and quicker, but we find driving to be relaxing, plus it gives us a great deal of time to converse. When we no longer have the responsibility of full-time work, one of our dream vacations is to drive from Michigan to southern California and follow the west coast into Canada. Along the way we will stay at spots of interest and enjoy some sights and scenery. But there will be many places we simply pass through.

There are times on our faith journey when God intends that we stay. There are also places He would never have us go. But then there are those infrequent occurrences when He leads us in, to only pass through.

Kevin and I have packed up our belongings and moved fourteen times in thirty-four years. It requires much organization and strategic planning to relocate. Though I do not mind packing and unpacking our household, I cannot imagine relocating a million-plus people.

And yet, Moses was ready to lead God's people out of Egypt. Moses had a plan and God paved the way. Remember, walking by faith walks all the way our Savior leads. God was saving His people, and He walked them to what appeared to be a dead end.

Surrounded by desert and mountains, that massive group stood at the shore of the Red Sea with the Egyptian army hot on their tails. There was also a shortcut available, but God does not take shortcuts. None were good options of escape, but only one was needed and God already had it planned: Pass through the Red Sea.

So God stacked water, dried up the sand, and, *by faith*, the people passed through on dry ground in the middle of the greatest aquarium exhibit the world has ever known. There was no stopping along the way to gawk at the underwater creatures floating by at eye-level; the people's assignment was to pass through.

And they did. Their responsibility was to walk by faith, not figure out what to do about the enemy closing in on them. God had their backs and placed a warring angel and a pillar of cloud between His people and the Egyptian army.

What exactly are passing-through moments? We cannot list them here because they are individual and personal. They may not always include hardship, but mine involve the sudden loss of a job, not knowing where we would live, cancer, friendship breaks, and more.

It was not up to me to try and fix, plan, or affect any of the outcomes of these situations. As a follower of Jesus, I was charged to walk by faith and pass through the hardship, trusting that God had my back, and He was leading me all the way through.

KEY POINT TO DAILY STAND: Walking in all God's ways sometimes requires passing through.

Day 19

Marching Orders

KEY VERSE: *By faith the walls of Jericho fell, after the people had marched around them for seven days.* Hebrews 11:30

It seems audacious and ludicrous to order God around, and yet, if we are honest, there are times our prayers appear to be ordering requests from a Sovereign and Almighty God, mimicking a fast-food experience.

We quickly and sometimes impulsively go to God, rattle off the things we need and expect of Him, and then a few minutes later, we are ready to receive our order. Heaven forbid, it does not meet our expectations or happen in a timely way!

Of course, that is a bit facetious, but it makes the point: Our prayers must be done by faith, and we are not the ones to give spiritual marching orders!

After Moses led the people out of Egypt, it was God's intent that they go to the Promised Land, but instead they wandered in the wilderness too long, and it had consequences. Even Moses died without leaving the wilderness. Then Joshua became the leader of God's people. The man has a book of the Bible named after him, and even though he walked by faith, he is not named in the Hall of Faith in Hebrews 11. But the people he led are mentioned.

What was the plan to take down the Jericho walls? March around the walled city for seven days. For the first six days, the orders were to march one time around with seven priests carrying trumpets. On the seventh day the same people were to march around, but the priests were to blow the trumpets and the people were to give a loud shout, and then the walls would come tumbling down!

The entry point to the Promised Land was the walled

city of Jericho. To take the city meant bringing the walls down.

The entry point for Jesus into our life is a walled heart. For Him to take control, management, and ownership, those walls must also come down.

Only God had a foolproof and perfect plan to bust down the walls of Jericho, and Joshua was entrusted with it. And only God made a way to take down the walls around a heart: His name is Jesus! (Interestingly, the Hebrew name for Joshua means, the Lord saves.)

My friend Jeanne is a warrior for Jesus. She loves her community in western Missouri. She prays for revival; she has opened her home for Bible studies and fellowship; she has organized, participated in, and gathered for prayer with friends, neighbors, and other Christians in her community.

Countless times Jeanne tells of the times she and other prayer warriors have gone to houses, businesses, and churches to pray, only she reports they did a *Jericho-drive-by*. She literally drives around a block or parking lot seven times while interceding for specific needs. Jeanne does not make the battleplan; she follows what God orders.

The power does not come from marching, shouting, trumpet blasts, or drive-bys; it only comes from the One who gives us our marching orders.

KEY POINT TO DAILY STAND: To walk by faith our marching orders are to walk in all God's ways.

Day 20

Unlikely Participant

KEY VERSE: *By faith the prostitute Rahab, because she welcomed the spies, was not killed with those who were disobedient.* **Hebrews 11:31**

    If we handpicked the participants in the bloodline to the Savior of the World, it is a high probability they would not possesses some of the problems, issues, character traits, habits, lifestyles, or reputations of the ones God chose. He handpicked Rahab. Not only is she in the Hall of Faith, but she is also one of five women named in the genealogy of Jesus.

    I have heard some complain about how the writer of Hebrews mentions her past profession. Frankly, they are misguided, most likely by unchecked feelings. Perhaps a change in perspective would help. Telling the reader she was a prostitute does not highlight her past profession; rather, it points to her testimony.

    Walking by faith means we should also be willing to tell others about who we were and how we lived before Jesus came into our lives, so that we can witness the change and transformation He brings to a person.

    Hebrews 11:31 explains what Rahab did *by faith* and how God honored her faithfulness:

- What she did: welcomed the spies.
- What God did: spared her life.

    At face value what Rahab did does not seem like it would have significant kingdom impact. However, regarding the kingdom of God, how things appear are not appropriate or accurate measuring tools. Her actions had immense and immeasurable impact!

Before the Israelite people could enter the Promised Land, Joshua called for a secretive reconnaissance mission and sent two spies to look over the land. So they went in and entered Rahab's house. Her home was in the city wall and after the king of Jericho heard about the spying, he sent messengers to Rahab to order the men to be brought out. But instead, she hid them until night and let them climb out the window so they could escape outside the city walls. Rahab pointed the king's men in a different direction (Joshua 2:1-7, 15).

Prior to the spies entering her house, God was already at work on her heart. She testified to the men about their God and how she knew the land belonged to them. She told them she had heard about the dried-up Red Sea and other things the Lord had done for His people. And then she pleaded with them on behalf of her family, "Please swear to me by the Lord that you will show kindness to my family…that you will save us from death" (Joshua 2:12-13).

Because she is in the genealogy of Jesus and honored for her faith in Hebrews 11, we know this prostitute was an unlikely participant in the saving of God's people and was indeed herself saved and changed by a promise-keeping, forgiving, redeeming, gracious, and Almighty God!

KEY POINT TO DAILY STAND: Do not underestimate the usefulness of unlikely participants in the spreading of the Gospel of Jesus Christ!

> "If you do not stand firm in your faith, you will not stand at all."
>
> Isaiah 7:9 b

Read before going to Day 21

A study through Old Testament champions of the faith, proves many were left out of Hebrews 11.

Can you relate?
Have you ever felt unrecognized or undervalued?
Your work or volunteerism for the Lord, unimportant or ignored?

In Hebrews 11:32 the writer names a few more heroes of the faith.
He writes, "I do not have time to tell about Gideon, Barak, Samson, Jephthah, David, Samuel, and the prophets, who through faith…"
Though they are named, specific attestations are not connected to their walk of faith.

The next eight daily readings come from bits of Hebrews 11:33-37.
The focus still includes by faith attestations, but without a Biblical hero attached.

Why?
Because there are people of God, past, present, and future, who live by faith without ever being lauded or applauded—and that is the way it ought to be—living by faith out of a love for God and an obligation to walk in all His ways.

Day 21

Conquerors

KEY VERSE: *...who through faith conquered kingdoms...Hebrews 11:33*

A *social media influencer* makes money; potentially, a lot of it. Which begs a question, what is their motivation—to impress or influence or to make money?
There is a difference between influencing others and impressing them.
Just because one calls themselves an influencer, does not mean they point people in the right direction. In today's Christian culture far too many influencers build platforms of followers and establish tribes of disciples while promoting themselves. Then *their* kingdom gets established, and *their* platform grows.
We are called to be disciples of Jesus and commissioned to make disciples for the transformation of the world. Hebrews 11:33 attests of some, "...who through faith conquered kingdoms..." We either conquer in the name of Christ or create a name for ourselves—we cannot have it both ways.
Old Testament heroes of faith conquered kingdoms, struggled against opposition, overcame hardship, and subdued powerful forces that came against them. Their faith journeys were not walks in the park; they were hard-fought fights of faith on difficult battlegrounds.
True conquerors fight the good fight of faith with kingdom mindsets, not minds set on establishing personal kingdoms. Christians are not merely conquerors; rather, Paul calls us *more than conquerors* (Romans 8:37).
Jesus conquered death by triumphing over the grave. Matthew Henry said we are more than conquerors, "...with little loss and great gain."

As we walk by faith, when it comes to facing hardship and dealing with difficulty, we need *more than* a conqueror mindset. Since we are in Jesus, we are more than conquerors! Are we to simply *grin and bear it* and just wait until better days come?

No!

Conquerors grin and bear whatever *it* is, but those who are more than conquerors, have Jesus as their role model. E. Stanley Jones, a missionary evangelist said, "Jesus did not bear the cross—He used it." Endurance is *more than* bearing—a Christian who endures, walks *by faith*, is more than a conqueror, allowing God to use whatever *it* is to bring glory, laud, and honor to Jesus.

The kingdom of God expands and others are influenced to live by faith when we walk in all God's ways as more than conquerors. Social media expansion is one way to influence people to Jesus, but we must be careful and intentional to have His kingdom on our minds. What better way is there than to be willing to be used by God to embrace difficulty and endure hardship as more than conquerors?

KEY POINT TO DAILY STAND: Conquering Christians commended for their acts of faith are to give all glory, laud, and honor to the Lord.

Day 22

Justice

KEY VERSE: *...who through faith administered justice...Hebrews 11:33*

In my personal life I coordinate calendars, organize tasks, maintain an orderly environment, manage our family's finances, run errands, and compartmentalize everyone's daily routine and specific whereabouts. However, since becoming a family thirty-four years ago, this has been a learned and practiced effort out of a necessity to avoid chaos. Though I have an appreciation for administration, I do not love it.

Though the word *administration* makes me uncomfortable and is not my strong suit, that cannot be an excuse to avoid the commendation of the faithful, found in Hebrews 11:33, to *administer justice*.

Creating a non-chaotic setting at home requires intentional administration but living by faith, demands we administer justice. Those who walk in all God's ways must perform, practice, and commit to living right—with integrity and correctness that is acceptable to God, in thinking, feeling, and action.

We can sum this up in one word: righteousness.

Administering justice lives right. It is that simple. Truly! God does not make living right a confusing or complicated matter. We do! We make it that way when we neglect, avoid, ignore, turn away, or refuse to live by faith.

Righteousness thinks, feels, and acts according to God's ways. He aptly sets standards; He properly determines behavior; He appropriately applies feelings. Holy justice must be administered in both our personal and public lives. God's idea of integrity is living right which is the same at home, in the community, at work, and in church.

As Christians, we pray for God's hand to move in many ways. We plead for healing and wholeness. We ask for restoration and open doors. We seek peace and joy. And we should pray for such things! But we ought to also implore the Lord to work His righteousness in us so we can daily live by faith. Matthew Henry, the great Bible commentator, said, "It is a greater honor and happiness to work righteousness than to work miracles."

We cannot live right without faith. Therefore, like the great heroes of the faith, we too, must administer justice. And we can only live in righteousness if we walk in all God's ways.

KEY POINT TO DAILY STAND: Living by faith lives right.

Day 23

Lions

KEY VERSE: *...who through faith shut the mouths of lions...Hebrews 11:33*

In the Old Testament, Samson, David, Daniel, and Benaiah each have separate events recorded about them regarding lions.

In Daniel's story he was sentenced to the lion's den for living by faith. But while there, an angel of the Lord shut the mouths of the beasts (Daniel 6:22). As a young shepherd, David, the future king of Israel went after lions and bears that approached his flock and stole sheep. After facing Goliath David told how he seized wild animals by their hair, struck them, and killed them (2 Samuel 17:34). And one day the Spirit of the Lord came upon Samson with power, and he tore a lion apart with his bare hands (Judges 14:6).

Benaiah's story is found in two verses of Scripture. 2 Samuel 23:20-21 says he was a valiant fighter describing how he struck down two of Moab's best men, how he used a club to take down a huge Egyptian wielding a spear, killing him with his own spear, and how he went down into a pit on a snowy day and killed a lion.

The two verses read like a warrior's resume that includes one astounding life event. And yet, it remains an obscure story, a hidden account of a brave and bold man who lived by faith.

It reminds me of us.

Most of us will not have a book written about us or even a mention in a history log of those who lived by faith. But what if we were asked to submit just one account from our faith journey showing a *shut-the-mouths-of-lions* act of faith? What testimony would we tell?

None of these four men had a lion experience without

living by faith. Whether God puts us on a public platform for many to hear our lion stories or our walk of faith remains obscure and hidden from most does not matter. To live *by faith* we must tuck in tight to the One who shuts the mouths of lions, who pours power into us to face the hardships in life, and who is with us as we face the giants that threaten our faith stance.

Before we fear the giants, we must look back to other *by faith* moments where God showed up and showed off in some wild trouble, meeting us in the pits of despair, dejection, distress, or despondency. Though living by faith may lead us into a pit, we can still know God's peace and sense His presence if we walk in all His ways.

KEY POINT TO DAILY STAND: How we walked by faith in the past bolsters us and builds strength to cooperate with God and witness Him shut the mouths of lions as we walk by faith today.

Day 24

Fire Extinguisher

KEY VERSE: *...who through faith quenched the fury of the flames...Hebrews 11:34*

If we are not careful, we could misinterpret or misread this *by faith* commendation. The three men referenced, but unnamed in today's key verse, did not put *out* a fire; rather, they thwarted and extinguished the powerful fear while standing *in* the fire!

The story of Shadrach, Meshach, and Abednego is told in the third chapter of Daniel. They were three godly, righteous, and devout men of God living in captivity in Babylon. The king of that pagan land had a ninety-foot-tall, nine-foot-wide golden image erected and he decreed that at the sound of many instruments everyone must bow down to the statue. The edict declared that anyone not worshiping the golden idol would be thrown into a blazing furnace.

In Daniel 3:12 the king hears, "There are some Jews…who pay no attention to you. They neither serve your gods nor worship the image…" The king was enraged and furious! He called the three men to his court and reminded them of his decree.

They responded, "…the God we serve is able to save us…we will not bow…"

The king raged with fury and ordered the three friends to be tied up and thrown into the fiery furnace, and he commanded the heat turned up seven times hotter. It was so hot it consumed and burned to death the soldiers who bound and threw the men into the fire!

The king leapt to his feet, shocked after he noticed four men, not three, unbound and unharmed walking around in the fire. When God enters our fury, all fear is gone!

God did not save the three men because their

situation was hot. No! He showed up and saved the men because they walked in all his ways—by faith—all the way into the fire. In the heat of the moment, the men were not concerned with the flames; they were consumed with hearts that burned out of a deep love of God and reverence for His glory! They were not consumed with fear; they were convinced God would meet them in the fire and extinguish any fury within them.

All too often we ask and expect God to extinguish the fires and get us out of hot situations when He is more concerned with settling the fury in our souls. Walking in all God's ways refuses to bow to cultural ideologies and is willing to take the heat for our faithful stance. As we trust the Lord to come alongside us, quenching the fear that might come, and extinguishing the fury of the flames, we live by faith.

KEY CHALLENGE TO DAILY STAND: Shadrach, Meshach, and Abednego were, "…willing to give up their lives rather than serve or worship any god except their own God," (Daniel 3:28). Are you?

Day 25

Weakness

KEY VERSE: ...*who through faith became powerful in battle and routed foreign armies. Hebrews 11:34*

Spiritual weakness happens. If we were strong, capable, deserved, and enough, then why would we need to live by faith? The truth is: we are not enough; we deserve death; we are not capable of attaining eternal life. Even the strongest, most resilient, and tenacious human is a mere weakling without Jesus.

We need Jesus! A favorite children's song from years past states, "Little ones to Him belong, they are weak, but He is strong," followed by the triad, "Yes, Jesus loves me." And it is His love that sustains and strengthens us in weakness. But because we may need to wait, or the trial looms on, or the testing of our faith is still enacted, we must walk by faith trusting in God's Word and His promises.

Samson was born to parents who for years could not have children, but God reversed the woman's barrenness for His good purposes. Before she conceived an angel of the Lord told her she would have a son and he would be set apart to God from birth and, "...begin the deliverance of Israel from the hands of the Philistines" (Judges 13:5).

When Samson was a boy, the Spirit of the Lord began to stir him to prepare and strengthen him for his future purpose preordained by God (Judges 13:25). But when Samson became a man, Judges 14:1 points to where his weakness began. Samson saw a woman from a land God forbade His people to intermingle with.

He saw her? What's the big deal? Seeing is not intermingling. No, but it was a step that distracted Samson from walking in all God's ways. And one step always leads to another when we are not tucked in tight to the Lord's strong arm. A step toward the forbidden stops us from walking in all God's ways. This *seeing* turned into an intermarriage that did not last.

Years later, Judges 16:1 proves where one step leads as it claims Samson saw a prostitute. Though the man had incredible human strength, he was flawed in his character. Samson had a weakness, and it affected his faith journey. He even intermarries again. Women were his weakness. Consequently, Samson suffered for not walking in all God's ways.

As we know God is a promise keeper, and he still used this one He had set apart from before birth. God began the deliverance of Israel anyway. One day all the Philistine rulers were partying and celebrating their god Dagon for delivering Samson into their hands. While the festivities increased, Samson prayed, "O Sovereign Lord, remember me. O God, please strengthen me just once more, and let me with one blow get revenge on the Philistines…" (Judges 16:28).

In his weakness, Samson called to God and God strengthened him. Samson pushed on the temple pillars with all his might, and the structure collapsed killing thousands of Philistines and one Israelite.

Yes, God still used Samson and strengthened him in his weakness, but what we do not know are all the ways God could not use Samson because, in his weakness, he did not walk in all God's ways.

KEY CHALLENGE TO DAILY STAND: Be careful where you step—it could lead to unforeseen outcomes and spiritual weakness.

Day 26

Rooted and Routed

KEY VERSE: *…who through faith became powerful in battle and routed foreign armies. Hebrews 11:34*

Stouthearted is not a commonly used characteristic trait. And yet, for those who walk by faith, it should be a well-known attribute. It is defined as brave, resolute, and dauntless. Here are two more words uncommonly used, and one wrongly applied.

Brave has been hijacked. We refer to many ordinary and expected actions as brave. We tell someone they are brave when they make an uncommon or surprising choice. I have been called brave when I changed my hair color and got a tattoo. Those choices required creativity and cash, not bravery.

Walking by faith grows roots. The deeper the roots, the stronger the rooted one becomes and the more powerful they are in battle. The original word for *powerful* means mighty and valiant in body and mind. To be battle-ready and to fight right, we must be valiant, which is stouthearted.

A brave Christian willingly goes to battle. A resolute follower of Jesus faces attacks head-on. A dauntless disciple fearlessly and boldly, but unintimidated, relies on the roots of faith buried in the fertile soil of their soul to rout opposition.

Living by faith recognizes that routing may be required. Sometimes we face the same hardship expecting to win battles assuming God works in ways He did before. But the writer of Hebrews does not say to walk by faith trusting God will do what He always does. No! Rather, he observes that those who live by faith are mighty in battle and ready to rout foreign armies—those things in our life that are hostile and not akin to the Family of God.

Remember we are called to live like aliens and strangers, but not necessarily apart from unbelievers. Yet, we are always supposed to live like we do not belong. We battle against cultural ideologies, inadequate influences, oppressive situations, worldly morals, manmade principles, family dynamics, relational dysfunction, and more!

For those who live by faith, a wise battleplan is to seek God's guidance to rout, or put to flight, those ungodly situations and oppressive circumstances that do not belong to a follower of Jesus.

Throughout the Old Testament we find accounts of God rerouting armies, putting to flight oppressive persons and nations who fled and fell before the faithful people of God.

Today, many churches and denominations struggle to keep and maintain the tenets of their faith. Perhaps it is because instead of being rooted in their faith and walking in all God's ways, they get established in the sinking sand of worldly values and cultural philosophies.

Living by faith is ready for all routed campaigns—using God's armament, trusting His battleplans, putting on His armor, and being rooted in Jesus.

KEY POINT TO DAILY STAND: Deep roots grow from hard battles. Hard battles are won through deep roots.

Day 27

Release Does Not Always Relieve

KEY VERSE: *...who through faith were tortured and refused to be released...Hebrews 11:35*

Right out of the gate, be prepared to focus on a word that makes us uncomfortable and uneasy. Ask the Lord to settle your soul to see His purpose in today's theme.

Torture. In today's key verse, the word for *tortured* is used only one time in Scripture. Its original meaning was to beat on a drum. It is where the phrase *beating to death* was derived. The problem with some words is that we impose assumptions. Yes, some torture is physical, but for Christians, we *must* apply it spiritually.

Spiritual torture? That does not seem like an uplifting theme for a daily reading. And yet, if we are willing to be candid, we have all experienced some form of it—enduring emotional hits, suffering mental attacks, bearing difficult burdens, and even tolerating personal assaults.

I have a friend who has recently undergone her share. Some would say she has had *more* than her share. But when it comes to spiritual torture, it is not appropriate to assert, or insert *more*—that implies it goes beyond God's awareness or His approval.

My friend takes hard hits for her firm and faithful stance working in a Christian industry that overwhelmingly tries to maneuver between worldly ways and following God's ways. Last week she reached out to me because of a recent beat down. This was my recent text to her:

Further study in Hebrews 11 has me in the middle of verse thirty-five with a message for you from the Lord. "...others were tortured and refused to be released..." Release does not always relieve. Goodness, _____, I'm beginning to see you as a modern-day martyr—one who suffers greatly—but for me, it goes a step further—one willing to suffer for the kingdom without seeking release SO THAT (here comes purpose) "...they might obtain a better resurrection." Martyr + Pioneer = necessary affliction to pave a path back to God's intended use. You know God is cleaning house, so maybe you are one of His ambassadors, called to not pray for release, but lean into Jesus for relief, steady and sturdily pressing on to take hits for a better resurrection of {the industry}. Praise God for your faithful stance!

So does God approve of His children taking a beat down? Yes, He does. Our perusal of Hebrews 11 supports it. But if we use human understanding and perspective, we will *never* see the kingdom's purpose or God's intended outcome.

Too often we fight the torture and cannot see God in it. We pray it away, begging God to make it go away. But the writer of Hebrews says those who live *by faith* refuse to be released because they focus on *a better resurrection*.

What if the hard hits—let us call it spiritual torture—were necessary? What if your emotional and mental anguish is used to stop a generational sin? What if *that* beat down you wished had never occurred is the very thing God used to reach your unsaved and lost friends or family?

KEY QUESTION TO DAILY STAND: What if we stopped praying for release and instead, asked Jesus to relieve us from the anguish of the torture so we could see it being used for His glory?

Day 28

Good News / Bad News

KEY VERSE: *...who through faith faced jeers and flogging...chained in prison...were stoned; sawed in two; put to death by the sword...destitute, persecuted, and mistreated...wandered in deserts and mountains, and in caves and holes...Hebrews 11:35-38*

If you thought yesterday's reading was deep, there might be hesitation to move on after reading today's key verses. But keep with it!

The other day I went into my dad's den (he lives with us) and told him I had good news and not-so-good news for him followed by, "Which would you like first?" He said, "I always begin with the Good News." (Capitalization, intentional.)

You see, with my dad everything begins with Jesus: decisions, diagnoses, and even, death. Dad is eighty-eight; he has more years behind than in front of him. Having Jesus as his foundation allows dad to navigate life and deal with the knowns, as well as the unknowns, of being an old man. Dad lives by faith.

Obviously, he has never been stoned, sawed in two, or put to death by the sword; nor has he been destitute or wandered in deserts and mountains, or spent time in caves and holes. But he has been persecuted and mistreated—not for martyrdom, but for Christendom.

As Christians the Good News must always be in our view. The sightline to bad news must have Jesus in view. He *is* the Good News! For those who claim to live by faith, it is imperative that bad news never outweighs, outdoes, overwhelms, or overcomes the Good News.

The unnamed saints mentioned in Hebrews 11:35-37 walked a faith journey *by faith.* Bad news did not stop them—Good News carried them, and this before Jesus came to Earth! They trusted the Lord—embracing His plan for their life and entrusting their journey to His control. Along their faith journey, every person alluded to in Hebrews 11:35-38 experienced immensely difficult and extremely trying times. But just because life was hard, does not mean it was bad.

Walking in all God's ways trusts that with God all things are possible, and He keeps His promises—before bad news comes, as bad news hits home, throughout the season of bad news, and when bad news is in the rearview mirror.

For us, bad things are not bad news. Oh, they may be challenging, cause suffering, bring trouble, and introduce hardship. We may lose friends, status, or jobs. We might need to go without some comforts, give up things we appreciate, or geographically relocate. Our reputations may take a hit; we might be disrespected, dissed, or disparaged.

But none of that is bad news when we personally know the Good News. Living by faith, willingly embraces bad news knowing we are being held, led, and loved by the Good News.

KEY POINT TO DAILY STAND: The Good News is the best news we will ever know!

Day 29

Broken Promises

KEY VERSE: *These were all commended for their faith, yet none of them received what had been promised.* **Hebrews 11:39**

When I was a teen girl, I had a boyfriend who made promises he did not keep. Do not feel bad for me. The promises did not match our age and were not realistic, let alone sincere.

When my kids approached dating age, I had certain conversations with them. One topic became necessary as I witnessed other parents treating the boyfriend/girlfriend break-up like a divorce.

In traditional wedding vows when the couple is pronounced *man and wife*, the pastor says something like, "What God has joined together, let nothing tear apart." The covenant of marriage is intact the moment God's representative declares it so. And what God put together, the Promise Keeper intends to hold it together.

When a boy and a girl, or a man and a woman date, and they break up, a natural separation occurs: two people go their separate ways. But in a covenant relationship of oneness, since two cannot be divided a split is unnatural.

God established covenant, but we did not; therefore, it must be lived out His way. The same is true for those who live by faith. The covenant we have with God now involves Jesus—as we read yesterday, He is the Good News and the foundation for our faith.

But for the saints who lived before Jesus came to Earth, they still walked by faith even though they never received what had been promised.

As the children of God, we have been promised eternal life spent in eternity with Jesus. Though we live on

Earth, because God will not back out on a covenant He enacted, the promise is still intact. Old Testament saints walked by faith without receiving the promise. We who walk by faith have received the Promise. The question is: do we live like it, or do some of our ways look as if we broke that promise?

KEY POINT TO DAILY STAND: Walk in all God's ways, living by faith, relying on the Promise Keeper.

Day 30

Something Better

KEY VERSE: *God had something better planned for us...Hebrews 11:40*

At one of the churches my husband served as pastor, he came up with a four-tiered visionary plan. He referred to two of those tiers as "good" and "better." The leadership of the church could see what was good and would have been content with it, but Pastor Kevin was leading *by faith*; therefore, he knew something better was in store for that congregation and led them beyond what they saw.

The writer of Hebrews concluded his *by faith* report with, "God had something better planned for us," on the heels of, "...yet none of them received what had been promised."

Which is better? Knowing something *will* be better or seeing that something indeed *is* better? Living by faith requires we trust that anything God plans is always something better even if we never see it or experience it.

Sometimes we believe something is not happening because we are not witnessing it. But God is always at work behind the scenes of His faithful followers.

For example, we consistently pray for someone who is lost. We ask Jesus to reveal Himself to that one; we plead for God to use us to plant seeds in their soul; we hope the Holy Spirit peels back the layers of doubt, fear, hesitation, or whatever it is that blinds them to surrendering to Jesus.

If we do not see our friend come to Jesus, do we give up? Do we think our witness was not good enough? God is clear in His Word: it is our duty to plant and water, but it is on Him to bring the harvest (1 Corinthians 3:6-7).

There is not one spiritual harvest we could bring that would ever be better than God's. He always has something better in store! The Old Testament saints who lived by faith never saw the promise fulfilled, but they pressed on knowing God had something better coming around the bend. Jesus came to Earth at the exact moment God planned; He carried His cross up Calvary's hill on the exact day God pre-planned; the Savior of the world died at the very second God ordered.

And something better happened on that one Easter morning than any other event in all of history or what is yet to come! Jesus conquered death! He rose from the grave! He lives for eternity!

And we get to celebrate Easter all year long! It does not get better than that!

KEY PROMISE TO DAILY STAND: There is nothing better than the *something better* God intended…for us!

Book by Ellen Harbin

CRISIS: falling to pieces was not an option for me

Proverbs 24:10 says, "If you fall to pieces in a crisis, there wasn't much to you in the first place." When God revealed that Scripture to Ellen, she had no idea she was about to face a major crisis in her life. But when she heard, "You have cancer," God brought this verse back to her memory.

CRISIS is Ellen's story and the lessons she learned when their adoption journey was interrupted by a cancer crisis.

STAND Bible Study series

STAND unashamed: identifying hidden shame & reclaiming identity

Ellen carefully confronts this often ignored and intimidating topic. Exposing the hidden places shame has taken over allows us to stand firm in our faith. This study is centered on some women in Genesis who are no different than us. If you are tired of being badgered with the same deception that shame must be accommodated and tolerated, then this study is for you!

STAND strong: face-to-face encounters with Jesus for the weary, the weak, and the worn out

Have the troubles in life depleted your strength? Through Ellen's candid style, you will relate to some individuals from the book of Mark who experienced troubles and trials. They were weary, weak, and worn-out! And just like them we need Jesus!

STAND ready: fighting right for the things worth fighting for

Have you ever felt unprepared to fight for something you knew was worth fighting for? Waiting until we are on the frontlines is not the time to figure out a battle plan. Too many people hope the issue will go away, but God wants us ready to face whatever comes our way.

STAND unmasked: wander well in the wilderness— revealing obstructions and outcomes that impede our walk with Jesus

What if instead of avoiding the wilderness we sought to wander well? Missteps, mishaps, and mistakes happen. Learn from Moses and the Israelites how to manage the space between hardship and promise.

CONTACT INFORMATION

Send an email to ellen@ellenharbin.com

- if you would like to keep updated on Ellen's speaking and writing

- if you are interested in having Ellen speak at your women's retreat, conference, or event

- if you would like to have Ellen as a guest (via Zoom, SKYPE, Google Meet, or a phone call) during one of your *STAND* Bible Study meetings

- if you would like to discuss hosting a *STAND women's conference* at your church or in your community

Find Ellen at ellenharbin.com

Follow Ellen on:
Facebook: facebook.com/ellenmharbin

ABOUT THE AUTHOR

Ellen Harbin is a gifted Bible teacher and conference speaker, creatively applying the truth of God's Word to everyday life. Ellen is the founder and visionary of the "STAND women's conference" based in Michigan. Through her teaching you will be encouraged to grow, challenged to change, and influenced to live as Jesus intends.

Ellen is married to Kevin and lives in Michigan. They have six children, three daughters-in-law, one son-in-law, and two grandchildren. Ellen loves deep conversations, laughing hard, spontaneous fun, sunrises, and quality time with friends.

Ellen says being a follower of Jesus is undeniably the best decision she has ever made.